botanical knits

TWELVE DESIGNS INSPIRED BY TREES AND FOLIAGE

By ALANA DAKOS of NEVER NOT KNITTING

NNK
PRESS

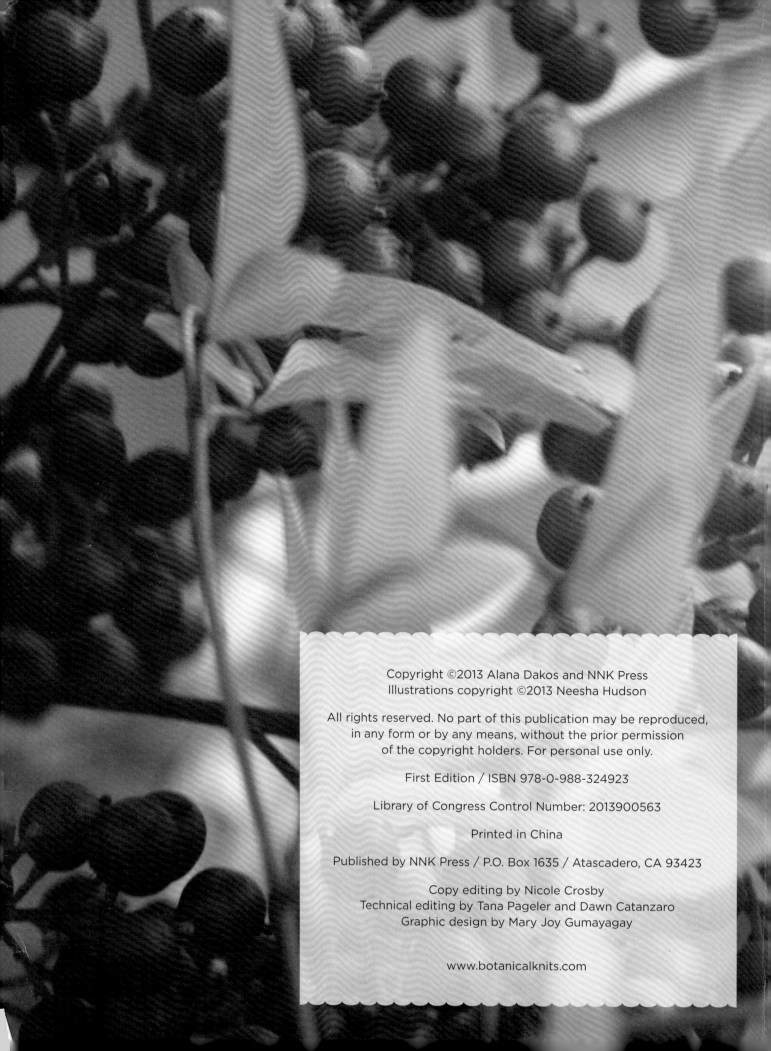

First Edition / ISBN 978-0-988-324923

Library of Congress Control Number: 2013900563

Printed in China

Published by NNK Press / P.O. Box 1635 / Atascadero, CA 93423

Copy editing by Nicole Crosby
Technical editing by Tana Pageler and Dawn Catanzaro
Graphic design by Mary Joy Gumayagay

www.botanicalknits.com

For J, A and O

with love

table of contents

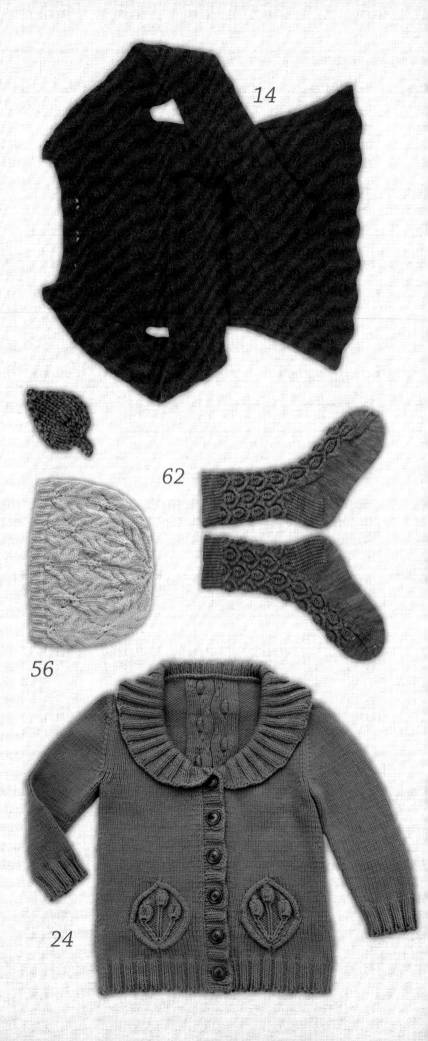

14

62

56

24

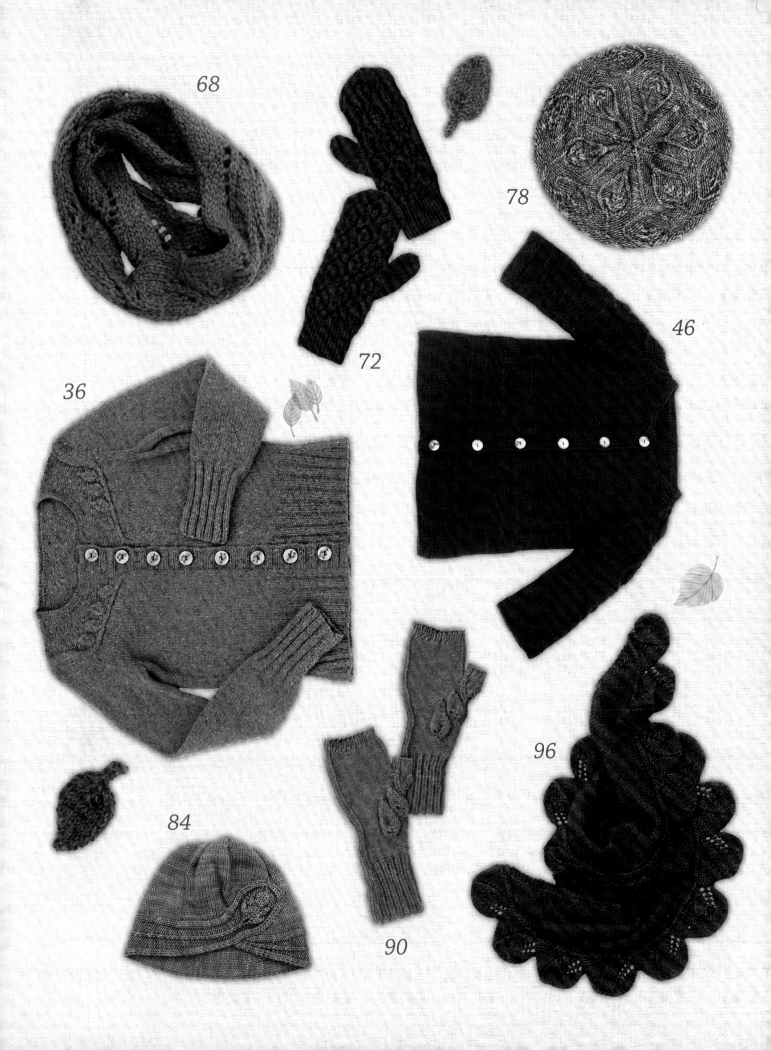

68

72

78

46

36

84

90

96

INTRODUCTION

I love leaves. I always have.

I don't know if it's because of the many nature walks my dad took me on as a child, or if it was growing up around the botanical murals my mother painted. Maybe it is being surrounded by beautiful oak trees and plant life here on the Central Coast of California. Perhaps it's a bit of all of these things. For as long as I can remember, I have been drawn to the natural beauty of leaves and plants.

In fact, it was this love of leaves and nature that inspired me to continue on in my knitting. I distinctly remember as a new knitter, sitting cross-legged in the craft section aisle of my local Barnes & Noble, poring over a particular stitch dictionary. As I flipped through the pages, I of course saw the traditional textured stitches, colorwork patterns, cables and then all of a sudden... leaves.

I had never even considered that leaf patterns could be worked into knitted fabric, and the thought of it absolutely fascinated me. I recall looking at a particularly beautiful knitted leaf edging and thinking to myself, "I will knit that one day." As a self-taught beginner at the time who barely knew how to work a purl stitch, the thought of this was a bit daunting.

I really do feel it was that gorgeous leaf edging, however, that kept me motivated to continue learning. Over the years, as I grew in my knowledge of knitting, my interest in plants and leaves greatly influenced my choice of knitting projects and my eventual design work. And as my skills increased, I did most certainly knit that edging. In fact, a version of that stitch pattern ended up adorning the bottom edge of one of my most popular shawl designs.

Incorporating botanical elements into stitch patterns is something I truly enjoy and it has

inspired me to create this new design collection, *Botanical Knits*.

This botanically inspired set of 4 sweaters and 7 accessories incorporates the beautiful colors, form and essence of plant life into a variety of knitted garments that I hope you will enjoy both knitting and wearing.

Elena

I KNOW YOU WANT TO GET YOUR NEEDLES AND YARN OUT AND CAST ON RIGHT THIS MINUTE... BUT WAIT! Before you begin, it is important to plan ahead to ensure the best possible outcome. Follow these steps now for a successful finished project later.

Choose the correct size.

Before beginning a sweater, you must first determine which size would be the best choice for a flattering fit.

At the beginning of each sweater pattern in this book, you will see the wide range of sizes listed as well as the recommended amount of "positive ease" (or extra room) the sweater should have when worn. You will want to add this amount of ease to your bust measurement to determine the correct size choice for you. The amount of ease listed is merely a recommendation, however. If you would prefer a tighter fit, add only 0–1" / 0–2.5 cm of positive ease. If you would like a roomier fit, add 3–4" / 7.5–10 cm. Once you determine the appropriate sweater size for your body, get out your measuring tape and compare your body measurements to the detailed schematic included in the pattern. This will help you to figure out how the finished piece will look when worn.

The sweater patterns included in this book follow the standard sizing guidelines, but not many of us are shaped in a "standard" way. Take the time to measure yourself and plan accordingly. You may need to go up or down a size, or shorten or lengthen the garment's body or sleeves.

Choose your yarn wisely.

If you would like to use a different yarn than the brands suggested for your project, there are a few important tips to keep in mind.

First, look at the fiber content. For the most reliable results, you will want to choose a yarn with a similar fiber content to the yarn used in the pattern. Different fibers act differently when knitted, washed and worn. A beautiful, shiny bamboo or silk might look gorgeous in the skein, but it may not translate well into a pattern that calls for a sturdy 100% wool or vice versa. Different yarns are suited for different applications, and careful consideration was given when matching yarn properties to garment design.

Additionally, you will want to choose a yarn that is the same weight and gauge as the recommended brand. One easy way to do this is to check the ball band for the following information:

- How many yards / meters in this skein?

- How many ounces / grams does this skein weigh?

- How many recommended stitches per inch?

Lastly, make a gauge swatch... or two... or ten.

You have probably heard this a million times, but you must, must, *must* check your gauge. Even if you are using the recommended yarn and needle size, you may knit much looser or tighter than the recommended gauge on the pattern.

We all knit differently. If you are off by just a little, it can mean inches of difference in a finished garment. Create a swatch that is at least 4" / 10 cm across. Be sure to bind off, wash, block, and dry your swatch before measuring how many stitches and rows you are getting per 1" / 2.5 cm. If the garment you are swatching for is knit in the round, knit your swatch in the round as well for the most accurate measurement. If your gauge is off, try again with another needle size until it is just right.

IF YOU FOLLOW THESE STEPS BEFORE BEGINNING, you will help to ensure your finished project looks the way you had hoped it would and fits your body in a flattering way. If you need help with your project, please join the Botanical Knits group on *Ravelry* where you will be able to share your questions and comments with other knitters who are creating the same items.

EVERY PATTERN IN THIS COLLECTION HAS BEEN TESTED AND CHECKED FOR ACCURACY by multiple technical editors prior to publishing. Despite our best efforts, however, sometimes errors can still slip by.

If you think you have found an error or have a question about a pattern instruction, please email techsupport@nevernotknitting.com and visit www.botanicalknits.com/errata for pattern corrections.

Happy Knitting!

P.S. Don't let those yarn scraps go to waste! Follow the trail of knitted leaves to find a pattern for all your leftover bits of yarn.

SWEATERS

autumn's end

The delicate leaf-lace stitch pattern makes this a perfect lightweight sweater for the transitional months. Waist shaping is worked in stockinette stitch on the sweater's sides producing a flattering contour. *Autumn's End* is worked from the bottom up in the round.

Body

Using long-tail cast on method, CO 172 (192, 212, 232)[252, 272, 292] sts onto largest circular needle.

Knit 1 RS row.

Pm, join for working in the rnd being careful not to twist your sts.

BORDER
Rnd 1: Purl 1 rnd.
Rnd 2: Knit 1 rnd.

Rep last 2 rnds once more.

Set up rnd: K71 (81, 91, 101)[111, 121, 131] front sts, pm, p2, k11, p2, pm, k71 (81, 91, 101)[111, 121, 131] back sts, pm, p2, k11, p2.

Switch to smaller circular needle.

Next rnd: {Work row 1 of Chart A over 71 (81, 91, 101)[111, 121, 131] sts, p2, k11, p2}, rep once more.

Work even in patt as est until piece measures 2½" / 6.5 cm from CO edge.

Dec rnd: {Work to marker, p2, ssk, knit to 4 sts before marker, k2tog, p2}, rep. 4 sts dec.

Rep dec rnd every 7 rnds, 3 times more. 156 (176, 196, 216)[236, 256, 276] sts.

Work even for 2" / 5 cm.

Inc rnd: {Work to marker, p2, k1, M1R, knit to 3 sts before marker, M1L, k1, p2}, rep. 4 sts inc.

Rep inc rnd every 7 rnds, 3 times more. 172 (192, 212, 232)[252, 272, 292] sts.

Cont as est until 92 (98, 92, 98)[104, 106, 108] chart rows have been completed, ending on row 12 (18, 12, 18)[4, 6, 8] of Chart A. Piece measures approx 14¾ (15¾, 14¾, 15¾)[16¾, 17, 17¼]" / 37.5 (40, 37.5, 40)[42.5, 43, 44] cm from CO edge.

Sleeves {MAKE 2}

Using long-tail cast on method, CO 46 sts onto largest circular needle.

Knit 1 RS row. Turn.

Divide sts evenly among 3 larger dpns. Pm, join for working in the rnd being careful not to twist your sts.

BORDER
Rnd 1: Purl 1 rnd.
Rnd 2: Knit 1 rnd.

Rep last 2 rnds once more.

Switch to smaller dpns.

Next rnd: K2, work row 7 (3, 17, 13)[9, 1, 13] of Chart A over 41 sts, k3.

Cont as est for 17 (11, 9, 7)[5, 5, 3] rows more.

Inc rnd: M1, work across row in est patt until 1 st rem, m1, k1.

Rep inc rnd every 18 (12, 8, 6)[4, 4, 2] rnds 4 (7, 11, 10)[3, 18, 4] times more, then every 0 (0, 0, 8)[6, 6, 4] rnds 0 (0, 0, 4)[14, 4, 23] times more, working additional sts in patt as they become available and always knitting last st of the rnd. 56 (62, 70, 76)[82, 92, 102] sts.

NOTE: To integrate extra sts into the lace patt, work extra sts in St st until there are 5 sts before and 6 sts after the sts worked in chart

patt. At the beg of the next rnd, shift the chart row you are working by 10 rows (e.g., skip from row 8 to row 18 or vice versa) and work all sts except the last st in the chart patt.

Cont as est until 106 rnds worked, ending on row 2 (8, 2, 8)[14, 16, 18] of Chart A. Sleeve measures approx 16¾" / 42.5 cm. Slide first 5 (6, 7, 8)[9, 10, 11] and last 6 (7, 8, 9)[10, 11, 12] sts onto a stitch holder for underarm. Slide the rem 45 (49, 55, 59)[63, 71, 79] sts onto a second stitch holder. Cut yarn leaving a long tail.

Yoke
JOIN SLEEVES TO BODY

Next rnd: K0 (5, 5, 5)[5, 5, 10], work row 13 (9, 3, 9)[15, 17, 9] of Chart A over 71 (71, 81, 91)[101, 111, 111] body sts, k0 (4, 3, 2)[1, 0, 4], p1, pm, p1, slide next 11 (13, 15, 17)[19, 21, 23] sts onto a stitch holder for underarm, k2 (4, 2, 4)[1, 0, 4] sts from first sleeve, work row 13 (19, 13, 9)[15, 17, 9] of Chart A over 41 (41, 51, 51)[61, 71, 71] sts, k2 (4, 2, 4)[1, 0, 4], p1 body st, pm, p1, k0 (4, 3, 2)[1, 0, 4], work row 13 (9, 3, 9)[15, 17, 9] of Chart A over 71 (71, 81, 91)[101, 111, 111] body sts, k0 (4, 3, 2)[1, 0, 4] sts, p1, pm, p1, slide next 11 (13, 15, 17)[19, 21, 23] sts onto a stitch holder for underarm, k2 (4, 2, 4)[1, 0, 4] sts from second sleeve, work row 13 (19, 13, 9)[15, 17, 9] of Chart A over 41 (41, 51, 51)[61, 71, 71] sts, k2 (4, 2, 4)[1, 0, 4], p1 body st, pm for new beg of rnd. 240 (264, 292, 316)[340, 372, 404] sts: 71 (79, 87, 95)[103, 111, 119] front/back sts, 45 (49, 55, 59)[63, 71, 79] sleeve sts, 8 raglan sts.

Next rnd: P1, work as est to end of rnd.

SIZES 34½ (42½, 46½)" / 87.5 (107.5, 118) CM ONLY
Begin raglan shaping over sleeve sts only.

Next rnd: {P1, k0 (3, 2), work row 15 (5, 11) of Chart A over 71 (81, 91) body sts to 1 (4, 3) sts before marker, k0 (3, 2), p1, sm, p1, work row 5 (15, 11) of Chart B over sleeve sts, p1}, rep.

Cont as est for 3 (7, 3) rnds more, ending on row 18 (12, 14) of Chart A over body sts and row 8 (2, 14) of Chart B over sleeve sts. 232 (276, 308) sts: 71 (87, 95) front/back sts, 41 (47, 55) sleeve sts, 8 raglan sts.

ALL SIZES

BEGIN RAGLAN SHAPING

Next rnd: {P1, work row 9 (1, 3, 15)[7, 19, 11] of Chart B over body sts, p1, sm, p1, work row 9 (1, 3, 15)[7, 19, 11] of Chart B over sleeve sts, p1}, rep.

Cont as est, switching to Chart C over sleeve sts after working row 20 of Chart B when 29 sleeve sts rem, until there are 51 (51, 61, 61)[61, 61, 61] front and back sts. End on chart row 8 of Chart B over body sts and row 8 of Chart C over sleeve sts. 152 (152, 172, 172)[172, 172, 172] sts: 51 (51, 61, 61)[61, 61, 61] front and back sts, 21 sleeve sts, 8 raglan sts.

NECK SHAPING

NOTE: Inc and dec must be worked in pairs in order to maintain st patt. If a complete pair cannot be worked, work sts in St st instead.

Next rnd: P1, work 21 sts in patt, BO 9 (9, 19, 19)[19, 19, 19] sts, cont in patt to end of rnd, then knit to end of row. 135 (135, 145, 145)[145, 145, 145] sts: 49 (49, 59, 59)[59, 59, 59] back sts, 20 front sts, 19 sleeve sts, 8 raglan sts.

Next row (WS): BO 10 sts purlwise, work row 10 of charts as est to end of row.

Next row (RS): BO 10 sts knitwise, cont in est patt to end of row. 107 (107, 117, 117)[117, 117, 117] sts: 47 (47, 57, 57)[57, 57, 57] back sts, 9 front sts, 17 sleeve sts, 8 raglan sts.

Work 1 WS row.

Dec row (RS): K1, ssk, work as est until 3 sts rem, k2tog, k1. 10 sts dec.

Rep dec row every RS row twice more. 77 (77, 87, 87)[87, 87, 87] sts: 41 (41, 51, 51)[51, 51, 51] sts, 3 front sts, 11 sleeve sts, 8 raglan sts.

Work 1 WS row.

Next row (RS): K1, k2tog, p1, work as est until 4 sts rem, p1, ssk, k1. 69 (69, 79, 79)[79, 79, 79] sts: 39 (39, 49, 49)[49, 49, 49] back sts, 2 front sts, 9 sleeve sts, 8 raglan sts. Remove markers.

Switch to smallest circular needle.

NECKBAND

With RS facing, pick up and knit 6 sts down left front side, 31 (31, 41, 41)[41, 41, 41] sts along center bound off sts, and 6 sts up the right front side. 112 (112, 132, 132)[132, 132, 132] sts.

Pm, and join into the rnd.

Rnd 1: Purl 1 rnd.
Rnd 2: Knit 1 rnd.

Rep last 2 rnds once more. Remove marker.

BO all sts purlwise.

Finishing

Slide held underarm sts onto 2 smaller dpns and graft sts together using the kitchener st. Use yarn tails to stitch up any rem holes. Weave in all ends on the WS. Wet block to measurements.

☐	knit RS rows, purl WS rows	◢	k2tog
⊡	purl RS rows, knit WS rows	◣	ssk
Ⓞ	yo	◪	k3tog
②	double yo	◩	sssk
⋁	kfb	⬆	S2KP2
⅜	Inc-3	▨	no stitch
⬇	knit RS rows, purl WS rows, then drop 2nd yo loop from needle	☐	patt rep

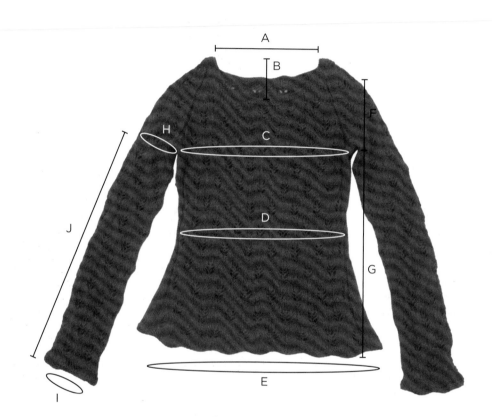

A	Back neck width	7¾ (7¾, 9¾, 9¾)[9¾, 9¾, 9¾]" 20 (20, 25, 25)[25, 25, 25] cm
B	Front neck depth	2¼" / 6 cm
C, E	Chest/hip circ	34½ (38½, 42½, 46½)[50½, 54½, 58½]" 87.5 (97.5, 107.5, 118)[128, 138, 148.5] cm
D	Waist circ	31¼ (35¼, 39¼, 43¼)[47¼, 51¼, 55¼]" 79 (89.5, 99.5, 109.5)[120, 130, 140] cm
F	Yoke depth	5¾ (6¼, 7½, 8)[8½, 9¾, 11]" 15 (16.5, 19, 20.5)[22, 25, 28] cm
G	Side length	14¾ (15¾, 14¾, 15¾)[16¾, 17, 17¼]" 37.5 (40, 37.5, 40)[42.5, 43, 44] cm
H	Upper arm circ	11¼ (12½, 14, 15¼)[16½, 18½, 20½]" 28.5 (31.5, 35.5, 38.5)[41.5, 46.5, 52] cm
I	Cuff circ	9¼" / 23.5 cm
J	Sleeve length	16¾" / 42.5 cm

Chart A

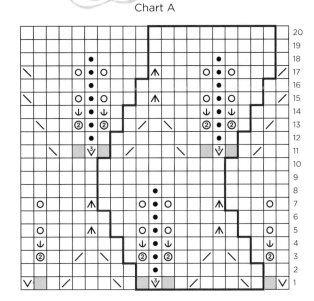

Chart B

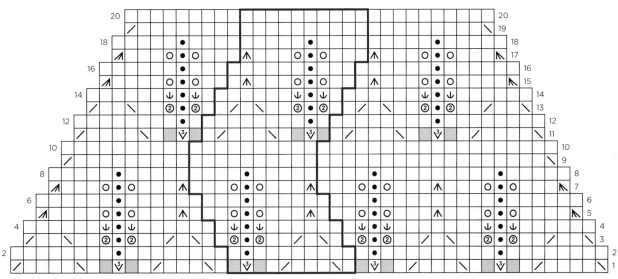

Chart C

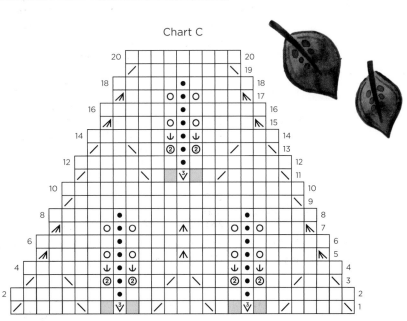

Chart A (WORKED IN THE ROUND)

(MULTIPLE OF 10 STS + 11)

Rnd 1: Kfb, {k1, ssk, k3, k2tog, k1, Inc-3}, k1, ssk, k3, k2tog, k1, kfb.

Rnd 2: K2, {k8, p1, k1}, k9.

Rnd 3: K1, double yo, k1, {k1, ssk, k1, k2tog, k2, double yo, p1, double yo, k1}, k1, ssk, k1, k2tog, k2, double yo, k1.

Rnd 4: K1, [knit double yo, dropping 2nd loop], k1, {k6, [knit double yo, dropping 2nd loop], p1, [knit double yo, dropping 2nd loop], k1}, k6, [knit double yo, dropping 2nd loop], k1.

Rnd 5: K1, yo, k2, {k1, S2KP2, k3, yo, p1, yo, k2}, k1, S2KP2, k3, yo, k1.

Rnd 6: K4, {k6, p1, k3}, k7.

Rnd 7: K1, yo, k3, {S2KP2, k3, yo, p1, yo, k3}, S2KP2, k3, yo, k1.

Rnd 8: K5, {k5, p1, k4}, k6.

Rnds 9 &10: Knit.

Rnd 11: K2, k2tog, k1, {Inc-3, k1, ssk, k3, k2tog, k1}, Inc-3, k1, ssk, k2.

Rnd 12: K4, {k1, p1, k9}, k1, p1, k5.

Rnd 13: K1, k2tog, k1, {k1, double yo, p1, double yo, k2, ssk, k1, k2tog, k1}, k1, double yo, p1, double yo, k2, ssk, k1.

Rnd 14: K3, {k1, [knit double yo, dropping 2nd loop], p1, [knit double yo, dropping 2nd loop], k6}, k1, [knit double yo, dropping 2nd loop], p1, [knit double yo, dropping 2nd loop], k4.

Rnd 15: K2tog, k1, {k2, yo, p1, yo, k3, S2KP2, k1}, k2, yo, p1, yo, k3, ssk.

Rnd 16: K2, {k3, p1, k6}, k3, p1, k5.

Rnd 17: K2tog, {k3, yo, p1, yo, k3, S2KP2}, k3, yo, p1, yo, k3, ssk.

Rnd 18: K1, {k4, p1, k5}.

Rnds 19 & 20: Knit.

Chart B (WORKED IN THE ROUND)

Rnd 1: Ssk, k4, k2tog, k1, Inc-3, {k1, ssk, k3, k2tog, k1, Inc-3}, k1, ssk, k4, k2tog.

Rnd 2: {K8, p1, k1}, k7.

Rnd 3: Ssk, k2, k2tog, k2, double yo, p1, double yo, k1, {k1, ssk, k1, k2tog, k2, double yo, p1, double yo, k1}, k1, ssk, k2, k2tog.

Rnd 4: {K6, [knit double yo, dropping 2nd loop], p1, [knit double yo, dropping 2nd loop], k1}, k5.

Rnd 5: Sssk, k4, yo, p1, yo, k2, {k1, S2KP2, k3, yo, p1, yo, k2}, k2, k3tog.

Rnd 6: {K6, p1, k3}, k3.

Rnd 7: Sssk, k3, yo, p1, yo, k3, {S2KP2, k3, yo, p1, yo, k3}, k3tog.

Rnd 8: K5, p1, k4, {k5, p1, k4}, k1.

Rnd 9: Ssk, knit to last 2 sts, k2tog.

Rnd 10: Knit.

Rnd 11: Ssk, k4, k2tog, k1, {Inc-3, k1, ssk, k3, k2tog, k1}, Inc-3, k1, ssk, k4, k2tog.

Rnd 12: K7, {k1, p1, k8}.

Rnd 13: Ssk, k2, k2tog, k1, {k1, double yo, p1, double yo, k2, ssk, k1, k2tog, k1}, k1, double yo, p1, double yo, k2, ssk, k2, k2tog.

Rnd 14: K5, {k1, [knit double yo, dropping 2nd loop], p1, [knit double yo, dropping 2nd loop], k6}.

Rnd 15: Sssk, k2, {k2, yo, p1, yo, k3, S2KP2, k1}, k2, yo, p1, yo, k4, k3tog.

Rnd 16: K3, {k3, p1, k6}.

Rnd 17: Sssk, {k3, yo, p1, yo, k3, S2KP2}, k3, yo, p1, yo, k3, k3tog.

Rnd 18: K1, {k4, p1, k5}.

Rnd 19: Ssk, knit to last 2 sts, k2tog.

Rnd 20: Knit.

Chart B (WORKED FLAT)

Row 1 (RS): Ssk, k4, k2tog, k1, Inc-3, {k1, ssk, k3, k2tog, k1, Inc-3}, k1, ssk, k4, k2tog.

Row 2 (WS): P7, {p1, k1, p8}.

Row 3: Ssk, k2, k2tog, k2, double yo, p1, double yo, k1, {k1, ssk, k1, k2tog, k2, double yo, p1, double yo, k1}, k1, ssk, k2, k2tog.

Row 4: P5, {p1, [purl double yo, dropping 2nd loop], k1, [purl double yo, dropping 2nd loop], p6}.

Row 5: Sssk, k4, yo, p1, yo, k2, {k1, S2KP2, k3, yo, p1, yo, k2}, k2, k3tog.

Row 6: P3, {p3, k1, p6}.

Row 7: Sssk, k3, yo, p1, yo, k3, {S2KP2, k3, yo, p1, yo, k3}, k3tog.

Row 8: P1, {p4, k1, p5}, p4, k1, p5.

Row 9: Ssk, knit to last 2 sts, k2tog.

Row 10: Purl.

Row 11: Ssk, k4, k2tog, k1, {Inc-3, k1, ssk, k3, k2tog, k1}, Inc-3, k1, ssk, k4, k2tog.

Row 12: {P8, k1, p1}, p7.

Row 13: Ssk, k2, k2tog, k1, {k1, double yo, p1, double yo, k2, ssk, k1, k2tog, k1}, k1, double yo, p1, double yo, k2, ssk, k2, k2tog.

Row 14: {P6, [purl double yo, dropping 2nd loop], k1, [purl double yo, dropping 2nd loop], p1}, p5.

Row 15: Sssk, k2, {k2, yo, p1, yo, k3, S2KP2, k1}, k2, yo, p1, yo, k4, k3tog.

Rnd 11: Ssk, k4, k2tog, k1, Inc-3, k1, ssk, k4, k2tog. 17 sts.

Rnd 12: K8, p1, k8.

Rnd 13: Ssk, k2, k2tog, k2, double yo, p1, double yo, k2, ssk, k2, k2tog.

Rnd 14: K6, [knit double yo, dropping 2nd loop], p1, [knit double yo, dropping 2nd loop], k6. 15 sts.

Rnd 15: Sssk, k4, yo, p1, yo, k4, k3tog. 13 sts.

Rnd 16: K6, p1, k6.

Rnd 17: Sssk, k3, yo, p1, yo, k3, k3tog. 11 sts.

Rnd 18: K5, p1, k5.

Rnd 19: Ssk, k7, k2tog. 9 sts.

Rnd 20: Knit.

Chart C (WORKED FLAT)

Row 1 (RS): Ssk, k4, k2tog, k1, Inc-3, k1, ssk, k3, k2tog, k1, Inc-3, k1, ssk, k4, k2tog. 27 sts.

Row 2 (WS): P8, k1, p9, k1, p8.

Row 3: Ssk, k2, k2tog, k2, double yo, p1, double yo, k2, ssk, k1, k2tog, k2, double yo, p1, double yo, k2, ssk, k2, k2tog. 29 sts.

Row 4: P6, [purl double yo, dropping 2nd loop], k1, [purl double yo, dropping 2nd loop], p7, [purl double yo, dropping 2nd loop], k1, [purl double yo, dropping 2nd loop], p6. 25 sts.

Row 5: Sssk, k4, yo, p1, yo, k3, S2KP2, k3, yo, p1, yo, k4, k3tog. 23 sts.

Row 6: P6, k1, p9, k1, p6.

Row 7: Sssk, k3, yo, p1, yo, k3, S2KP2, k3, yo, p1, yo, k3, k3tog. 21 sts.

Row 8: P5, k1, p9, k1, p5.

Row 9: Ssk, knit to last 2 sts, k2tog. 19 sts.

Row 10: Purl.

Row 11: Ssk, k4, k2tog, k1, Inc-3, k1, ssk, k4, k2tog. 17 sts.

Row 12: P8, k1, p8.

Row 13: Ssk, k2, k2tog, k2, double yo, p1, double yo, k2, ssk, k2, k2tog.

Row 14: P6, [purl double yo, dropping 2nd loop], k1, [purl double yo, dropping 2nd loop], p6. 15 sts.

Row 15: Sssk, k4, yo, p1, yo, k4, k3tog. 13 sts.

Row 16: P6, k1, p6.

Row 17: Sssk, k3, yo, p1, yo, k3, k3tog. 11 sts.

Row 18: P5, k1, p5.

Row 19: Ssk, k7, k2tog. 9 sts.

Row 20: Purl.

Row 16: {P6, k1, p3}, p3.

Row 17: Sssk, {k3, yo, p1, yo, k3, S2KP2}, k3, yo, p1, yo, k3, k3tog.

Row 18: {P5, k1, p4}, p1.

Row 19: Ssk, knit to last 2 sts, k2tog.

Row 20: Purl.

Chart C (WORKED IN THE ROUND)

Rnd 1: Ssk, k4, k2tog, k1, Inc-3, k1, ssk, k3, k2tog, k1, Inc-3, k1, ssk, k4, k2tog. 27 sts.

Rnd 2: K8, p1, k9, p1, k8.

Rnd 3: Ssk, k2, k2tog, k2, double yo, p1, double yo, k2, ssk, k1, k2tog, k2, double yo, p1, double yo, k2, ssk, k2, k2tog. 29 sts.

Rnd 4: K6, [knit double yo, dropping 2nd loop], p1, [knit double yo, dropping 2nd loop], k7, [knit double yo, dropping 2nd loop], p1, [knit double yo, dropping 2nd loop], k6. 25 sts.

Rnd 5: Sssk, k4, yo, p1, yo, k3, S2KP2, k3, yo, p1, yo, k4, k3tog. 23 sts.

Rnd 6: K6, p1, k9, p1, k6.

Rnd 7: Sssk, k3, yo, p1, yo, k3, S2KP2, k3, yo, p1, yo, k3, k3tog. 21 sts.

Rnd 8: K5, p1, k9, p1, k5.

Rnd 9: Ssk, knit to last 2 sts, k2tog. 19 sts.

Rnd 10: Knit.

buds and blooms

A warm and cozy jacket complete with a rounded fold-over collar and ¾-length sleeves. A budding vine stalk climbs up the back and adorns the circular pockets. The jacket is worked in pieces from the bottom up and seamed together at the end; the pockets are joined as you knit the jacket fronts.

{ FINISHED MEASUREMENTS }

Chest: 34 (38, 42, 46)[50, 54, 58, 62]" /
86.5 (96.5, 106.5, 117)[127, 137, 147.5, 157.5] cm
Length: 21½ (22½, 23½, 24½)[25½, 26½, 27½, 28½]" /
54.5 (57, 59.5, 62)[64.5, 67, 69.5, 72] cm
Shown in size 34" / 86.5 cm
To be worn with 2–3" / 5–7.5 cm of positive ease.

{ MATERIALS }

6 (7, 8, 8)[9, 10, 11, 11] skeins Quince & Co. *Osprey*
[100% American Wool; 170 yd / 155 m per 3½ oz /
100 g skein] in Twig OR approx 950 (1075, 1225, 1325)
[1475, 1600, 1750, 1875] yd / 875 (975, 1100, 1200)[1350,
1450, 1600, 1725] m of a bulky weight wool or wool blend

Alternate Yarn: Cascade Yarns *Ecological Wool*

US9 / 5.5 mm 32" / 80 cm circular needle
US8 / 5 mm 32" / 80 cm circular needle
and 3 dpns for three-needle bind off

Stitch markers, stitch holders, cable needle,
tapestry needle, 6 buttons 1" / 2.5 cm diameter,
sewing needle and matching thread

{ GAUGE }

16 sts and 22 rows over 4" / 10 cm in St st
on US9 / 5.5 mm needles
Or size needed for accurate gauge.

Back

CO 75 (83, 91, 99)[107, 115, 123, 131] sts onto larger circular needle.

Ribbing setup row (WS): P3, k2, {p2, k2} 8 (9, 10, 11)[12, 13, 14, 15] times total, p1, {k2, p2} 8 (9, 10, 11)[12, 13, 14, 15] times total, k2, p3.

Work even in est rib patt until work measures 2" / 5 cm from CO edge. End with a WS row.

Setup row (RS): K31 (35, 39, 43)[47, 51, 55, 59], pm, work Chart A over next 13 sts, pm, k31 (35, 39, 43)[47, 51, 55, 59].

Work 1 WS row even in est patt working St st on either side of chart patt.

Dec row (RS): K2, ssk, work across row in est patt until 4 sts rem, k2tog, k2. 2 sts dec.

Work even as est, working Chart A patt over center sts and St st on either side of chart patt. Rep dec row when work measures 4½" / 11.5 cm from CO edge and again when work measures 9" / 23 cm

from CO edge. 28 (32, 36, 40)[44, 48, 52, 56] sts on each side of chart patt section.

Work even as est until work measures 14½ (15, 15½, 16)[16½, 17, 17½, 18]" / 37 (38, 39.5, 40.5)[42, 43, 44.5, 45.5] cm from CO edge. End with a WS row.

ARMHOLE SHAPING

BO 3 (4, 5, 6)[7, 8, 9, 10] sts at beg of next 2 rows, then 0 (0, 0, 2)[3, 4, 5, 6] sts at beg of next 0 (0, 0, 2)[2, 2, 2, 2] rows.

Dec row (RS): K2, ssk, work across row in est patt until 4 sts rem, k2tog, k2. 2 sts dec.

Rep dec row every RS row 1 (2, 4, 4)[5, 6, 7, 8] time(s) more. 23 (25, 26, 27)[28, 29, 30, 31] sts on each side of chart patt section.

Work even as est until armhole measures 6½ (7, 7½, 8)[8½, 9, 9½, 10]" / 16.5 (18, 19, 20.5)[21.5, 23, 24, 25.5] cm. End with a WS row.

SHOULDER SHAPING

NOTE: When working the following rows, end chart on row 18 or 26, then work 15 chart sts as they appear from that point forward.

Short Row 1 (RS): Knit until 5 (6, 5, 5)[6, 6, 7, 7] sts rem, w&t.
Short Row 2 (WS): Purl until 5 (6, 5, 5)[6, 6, 7, 7] sts rem, w&t.
Short Row 3 (RS): Knit until 5 (5, 6, 6)[6, 6, 6, 6] sts rem from last wrapped st, w&t.
Short Row 4 (WS): Purl until 5 (5, 6, 6)[6, 6, 6, 6] sts rem from last wrapped st, w&t.

Rep short rows 3 and 4 once more.

Next row (RS): Work across row in patt picking up and knitting wraps as you go.
Next row (WS): Work across row in patt picking up and purling wraps as you go.
Next row (RS): K15 (16, 17, 17)[18, 18, 19, 19] shoulder sts, BO until 14 (15, 16, 16)[17, 17, 18, 18] sts rem, knit to end.

Cut yarn leaving a long tail. Slide unworked shoulder sts onto 2 separate holders to be worked later. 15 (16, 17, 17)[18, 18, 19, 19] sts rem for each shoulder.

Left Front

CO 36 (40, 44, 48)[52, 56, 60, 64] sts onto larger circular needle.

Ribbing setup row (WS): P1, {k2, p2}, rep until 3 sts rem, k2, p1.

Work even in est rib patt until piece measures 2" / 5 cm from CO edge. End with a WS row.

Knit 1 RS row.

Purl 1 WS row.

Cont in St st.

Dec row (RS): K2, ssk, knit to end. 35 (39, 43, 47)[51, 55, 59, 63] sts.

Purl 1 WS row.

Pocket Setup row (RS): K9 (13, 17, 21)[25, 29, 33, 37], pm, work Chart B over next 21 sts, pm, k5.

Cont in est patt, working rows 1–12 between markers and St st on either side of chart patt.

Next row (RS): K2, ssk, work in est patt to end. 36 (40, 44, 48)[52, 56, 60, 64] sts.

Next row: P5, work chart row 14 over 23 sts, slide rem 8 (12, 16, 20) [24, 28, 32, 36] sts on holder for side front. 28 sts.

Work rows 15–18 of Chart B, then work rows 1–13 of Chart C. Do not cut yarn. Slide rem 15 sts on holder for center front.

Left Pocket Lining

With a separate ball of yarn, CO 5 sts onto larger circular needle.

Row 1 and all WS rows: Purl.
Row 2 (RS): {K1, M1R} twice, {K1, M1L} twice, k1. 9 sts.
Row 4: {K1, M1R} twice, k5, {M1L, k1} twice. 13 sts.
Row 6: K1, M1R, knit until 1 st rem, M1L, k1. 2 sts inc.
Rows 8 & 10: As for row 6. 19 sts.
Row 12: K1, M1R, knit until 1 st rem, M1L, k1. 21 sts.

Slide 8 (12, 16, 20)[24, 28, 32, 36] side front sts from holder onto needle, ready to work a WS row.

Next row (WS): Work 21 pocket lining sts, work 8 (12, 16, 20)[24, 28, 32, 36] side front sts. 29 (33, 37, 41)[45, 49, 53, 57] sts.

Work even in St st for 6 rows more.

Dec row (RS): Knit until 3 sts rem, k2tog, k1. 1 st dec.

Rep dec row every RS row twice more. 26 (30, 34, 38)[42, 46, 50, 54] sts.

Purl 1 WS row.

Dec row (RS): Knit until 5 sts rem, k2tog twice, k1. 2 sts dec.

Rep dec row every RS row twice more. 20 (24, 28, 32)[36, 40, 44, 48] sts.

Work even in St st for 2 rows more. End with a RS row.

Cut yarn. Slide 15 center front sts onto needle ready to work a WS row.

Next row (WS): Purl 15 center front sts, then purl 20 (24, 28, 32) [36, 40, 44, 48] side front sts. 35 (39, 43, 47)[51, 55, 59, 63] sts.

Work even in St st until piece measures 9" / 23 cm from CO edge. End with a WS row.

Next row (RS): K2, ssk, knit to end. 34 (38, 42, 46)[50, 54, 58, 62] sts.

Work even in St st until piece measures 14½ (15, 15½, 16)[16½, 17, 17½, 18]" / 37 (38, 39.5, 40.5)[42, 43, 44.5, 45.5] cm from CO edge. End with a WS row.

ARMHOLE SHAPING

BO 3 (4, 5, 6)[7, 8, 9, 10] sts at beg of next RS row, then 0 (0, 0, 2)[3, 4, 5, 6] sts at beg of next 0 (0, 0, 1)[1, 1, 1, 1] RS row.

Work 1 WS row even.

Dec row (RS): K2, ssk, knit to end. 1 st dec.

Rep dec row every RS row 1 (2, 4, 4)[5, 6, 7, 8] time(s) more. 29 (31, 32, 33)[34, 35, 36, 37] sts.

When armhole measures 1 (1½, 2, 2½)[3, 3½, 4, 4½]" / 2.5 (4, 5, 6.5) [7.5, 9, 10, 11.5] cm, shape neckline as follows:

BO 6 sts purlwise at beg of next WS row.

Dec row (RS): Knit until 4 sts rem, k2tog, k2. 1 st dec.

Rep dec row every RS row 7 (8, 8, 9)[9, 10, 10, 11] times more. 15 (16, 17, 17)[18, 18, 19, 19] sts.

Work even in St st until armhole measures 6½ (7, 7½, 8)[8½, 9, 9½, 10]" / 16.5 (18, 19, 20.5)[21.5, 23, 24, 25.5] cm. End with a RS row.

SHOULDER SHAPING

Short Row 1 (WS): Purl until 5 (5, 6, 6)[6, 6, 6, 6] sts rem, w&t.
Short Row 2 (RS): Knit to end.
Short Row 3 (WS): Purl until 4 (4, 5, 5)[5, 5, 5, 5] sts rem from last wrapped st, w&t.
Short Row 4 (RS): Knit to end.

Next row (WS): Purl across row picking up and purling wraps as you go.

Cut yarn. Slide shoulder sts onto a st holder to be worked later.

Right Front

CO 36 (40, 44, 48)[52, 56, 60, 64] sts onto larger circular needle.

Ribbing setup row (WS): P1, {k2, p2}, rep until 3 sts rem, k2, p1.

Work even in est rib patt until piece measures 2" / 5 cm from CO edge. End with a WS row.

Knit 1 RS row.

Purl 1 WS row.

Cont in St st.

Dec row (RS): Knit until 4 sts rem, k2tog, k2. 35 (39, 43, 47)[51, 55, 59, 63] sts.

Purl 1 WS row.

Pocket Setup row (RS): K5, pm, work Chart B over next 21 sts, pm, k9 (13, 17, 21)[25, 29, 33, 37].

Cont in est patt, working rows 1–12 between markers and St st on either side of chart patt.

Next row (RS): K5, work row 13 over 23 sts, slide rem 9 (13, 17, 21) [25, 29, 33, 37] sts on holder for side front. 28 sts.

Work rows 14–18 of Chart B, then work rows 1–13 of Chart D. Cut yarn. Slide rem 15 sts on holder for center front.

Right Pocket Lining

With a separate ball of yarn, CO 5 sts onto larger circular needle.

Row 1 and all WS rows: Purl.
Row 2 (RS): {K1, M1R} twice, {K1, M1L} twice, k1. 9 sts.
Row 4: {K1, M1R} twice, k5, {M1L, k1} twice. 13 sts.
Row 6: K1, M1R, knit until 1 st rem, M1L, k1. 2 sts inc.
Rows 8 & 10: As for row 6. 19 sts.
Row 12: K1, M1R, knit until 1 st rem, M1L, k1. 21 sts.

Purl 1 WS row.

Slide 9 (13, 17, 21)[25, 29, 33, 37] side front sts from holder onto needle, ready to work a RS row.

Next row (RS): Work 21 pocket lining sts, work 5 (9, 13, 17)[21, 25, 29, 33] side front sts, k2tog, k2. 29 (33, 37, 41)[45, 49, 53, 57] sts.

Work even in St st for 5 rows more.

Dec row (RS): K1, ssk, knit to end. 1 st dec.

Rep dec row every RS row twice more. 26 (30, 34, 38)[42, 46, 50, 54] sts.

Purl 1 WS row.

Dec row (RS): K1, ssk twice, knit to end. 2 sts dec.

Rep dec row every RS row twice more. 20 (24, 28, 32)[36, 40, 44, 48] sts.

Work even in St st for 2 rows more. End with a RS row.

Slide 15 center front sts onto needle ready to work a WS row.

Next row (WS): Purl 20 (24, 28, 32)[36, 40, 44, 48] side front sts, then purl 15 center front sts. 35 (39, 43, 47)[51, 55, 59, 63] sts.

Work even in St st until piece measures 9" / 23 cm from CO edge. End with a WS row.

Next row (RS): Work until 4 sts rem, k2tog, k2. 34 (38, 42, 46)[50, 54, 58, 62] sts.

Work even in St st as est until piece measures 14½ (15, 15½, 16) [16½, 17, 17½, 18]" / 37 (38, 39.5, 40.5)[42, 43, 44.5, 45.5] cm from CO edge. End with a RS row.

ARMHOLE SHAPING

BO 3 (4, 5, 6)[7, 8, 9, 10] sts at beg of next WS row, then 0 (0, 0, 2)[3, 4, 5, 6] sts at beg of next 0 (0, 0, 1)[1, 1, 1, 1] WS row(s).

Dec row (RS): Knit until 4 sts rem, k2tog, k2. 1 st dec.

Rep dec row every RS row 1 (2, 4, 4)[5, 6, 7, 8] time(s) more. 29 (31, 32, 33)[34, 35, 36, 37] sts.

When armhole measures 1 (1½, 2, 2½)[3, 3½, 4, 4½]" / 2.5 (4, 5, 6.5) [7.5, 9, 10, 11.5] cm, shape neckline as follows:

BO 6 sts at beg of next RS row.

Purl 1 WS row.

Dec row (RS): K2, ssk, knit to end. 1 st dec.

Rep dec row every RS row 7 (8, 8, 9)[9, 10, 10, 11] times more. 15 (16, 17, 17)[18, 18, 19, 19] sts.

Work even in St st until armhole measures 6½ (7, 7½, 8)[8½, 9, 9½, 10]" / 16.5 (18, 19, 20.5)[21.5, 23, 24, 25.5] cm. End with a WS row.

SHOULDER SHAPING

Short Row 1 (RS): Knit until 5 (5, 6, 6)[6, 6, 6, 6] sts rem, w&t.
Short Row 2 (WS): Purl to end.
Short Row 3 (RS): Knit until 4 (4, 5, 5)[5, 5, 5, 5] sts rem from last wrapped st, w&t.
Short Row 4 (WS): Purl to end.

Next row (RS): Knit across row picking up and knitting wraps as you go.

Cut yarn. Slide shoulder sts onto a st holder to be worked later.

Sleeves (MAKE 2)

CO 38 (38, 42, 42)[46, 46, 50, 50] sts onto larger circular needle.

Ribbing setup row (WS): P2, {k2, p2}, rep.

Work even in est rib patt for 2" / 5 cm from CO edge. End with a WS row.

Knit 1 RS row.

Cont in St st as est for 7 (5, 3, 3)[3, 1, 1, 1] row(s) more. End with a WS row.

Inc row (RS): K2, M1R, knit to last 2 sts, M1L, k2. 2 sts inc.

Rep inc row every 8 (6, 4, 4)[4, 2, 2, 2] rows 4 (6, 2, 7)[10, 3, 5, 9] times more, then every 0 (0, 6, 6)[0, 4, 4, 4] rows 0 (0, 5, 2)[0, 9, 8, 6] times more. 48 (52, 58, 62)[68, 72, 78, 82] sts.

Work even in St st until sleeve measures 11" / 28 cm from CO edge. End with a WS row.

SLEEVE CAP SHAPING

BO 3 (4, 5, 6)[7, 8, 9, 10] sts at beg of next 2 rows then 0 (0, 0, 2)[3, 4, 5, 6] sts at beg of next 0 (0, 0, 2)[2, 2, 2, 2] rows.

Dec row (RS): K1, ssk, knit until 3 sts rem, k2tog, k1. 2 sts dec.

Rep dec row every RS row 1 (2, 4, 4)[5, 6, 7, 8] time(s) more, then every 4th row 1 (1, 1, 2)[2, 4, 4, 5] time(s) more, then every RS row 9 (9, 9, 7)[7, 4, 4, 2] times more. 18 sts.

Purl 1 WS row.

BO 2 sts at beg of next 2 rows.

BO 3 sts at beg of next 2 rows.

BO rem 8 sts. Cut yarn.

Finishing
BUTTON BAND

With smaller circular needle and RS facing, beg at the neck edge of left front and pick up and knit 71 (71, 75, 75)[79, 79, 83, 83] sts along left front edge.

Ribbing setup row (WS): {P2, k2} rep until 3 sts rem, p3.

Cont in est rib patt for 8 rows more. End with a WS row.

BO all sts in rib.

BUTTONHOLE BAND

With smaller circular needle and RS facing, beg at the bottom CO edge of right front and pick up and knit 71 (71, 75, 75)[79, 79, 83, 83] sts along right front edge.

Ribbing setup row (WS): P3, {k2, p2}, rep to end.

Cont in est rib patt for 3 rows more.

Buttonhole row (WS): P3, {work one-row buttonhole, work 10 (10, 10, 10)[11, 11, 12, 12] sts in patt}, 4 (4, 1, 1)[2, 2, 3, 3] time(s) total, then {work one-row buttonhole, work 10 (10, 11, 11)[12, 12, 13, 13] sts in patt}, 1 (1, 4, 4)[3, 3, 2, 2] time(s) total, work one-row buttonhole once more, p2, k2, p2.

Cont in est rib patt for 4 rows more. End with a WS row.

BO all sts in rib.

Return shoulder sts to spare dpns and seam shoulder sts together using three-needle bind off method.

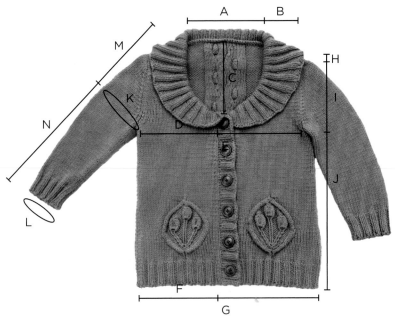

A	Back neck width	7¾ (8¼, 8¼, 8¾)[8¾, 9¼, 9¼, 9¾]" 19.5 (21, 21, 22)[22, 23.5, 23.5, 25] cm
B	Shoulder width	3¾ (4, 4¼, 4¼)[4½, 4½, 4¾, 4¾]" 9.5 (10, 11, 11)[11.5, 11.5, 12, 12] cm
C	Neck depth	5¾" / 15 cm
D	Front chest width*	8½ (9½, 10½, 11½)[12½, 13½, 14½, 15½]" 21.5 (24, 26.5, 29)[32, 34.5, 37, 39.5] cm
E	Back chest width	17½ (19½, 21½, 23½)[25½, 27½, 29½, 31½]" 44.5 (49.5, 54.5, 59.5)[65, 70, 75, 80] cm
F	Front hip width*	9 (10, 11, 12)[13, 14, 15, 16]" 23 (25.5, 28, 30.5)[33, 35.5, 38, 40.5] cm
G	Back hip width	18¾ (20¾, 22¾, 24¾)[26¾, 28¾, 30¾, 32¾]" 47.5 (52.5, 58, 63)[68, 73, 78, 83] cm
H	Shoulder height	1" / 2.5 cm
I	Armhole depth	6¾ (7¼, 7¾, 8¼)[8¾, 9¼, 9¾, 10¼]" 17.5 (18.5, 20, 21)[22.5, 24, 25, 26.5] cm
J	Side length	14½ (15, 15½, 16)[16½, 17, 17½, 18]" 37 (38, 39.5, 40.5)[42, 43, 44.5, 45.5] cm
K	Upper arm circ	12 (13, 14½, 15½)[17, 18, 19½, 20½]" 30.5 (33, 37, 39.5)[43, 45.5, 49.5, 52] cm
L	Cuff circ	9½ (9½, 10½, 10½)[11½, 11½, 12½, 12½]" 24 (24, 26.5, 26.5)[29, 29, 32, 32] cm
M	Cap height	5½ (5¾, 6½, 7)[7¼, 8, 8¼, 8¾]" 14 (15, 16.5, 17.5)[18.5, 20.5, 21, 22] cm
N	Sleeve length	11" / 28 cm

* measurement does not include button band

COLLAR

With smaller circular needle and RS facing, beg at the start of neck shaping on the right front and pick up and knit 33 sts along neck edge to right shoulder seam, 33 (36, 36, 36)[36, 39, 39, 42] sts along back neck, 33 sts to beg of neck edge dec rows on left front. 99 (102, 102, 102)[102, 105, 105, 108] sts.

Row 1 (RS): {K1, p1, k1}, rep to end.
Row 2: P1, M1-p, work even in est rib patt until 1 st rem, M1-p, p1. 101 (104, 104, 104)[104, 107, 107, 110] sts.
Row 3: K1, {k1, p1, k1}, rep until 1 st rem, k1.
Row 4: P1, M1-p, work even in est rib patt until 1 st rem, M1-p, p1. 103 (106, 106, 106)[106, 109, 109, 112] sts.
Row 5: K2, {k1, p1, k1}, rep until 2 sts rem, k2.
Row 6: P1, M1L, work even in est rib patt until 1 st rem, M1L, p1. 105 (108, 108, 108)[108, 111, 111, 114] sts.
Row 7: {K1, p1, k1}, rep to end.
Row 8: P1, M1L, k1, p1, {p1, kfb, p1}, rep until 3 sts rem, p1, k1, M1R, p1. 140 (144, 144, 144)[144, 148, 148, 152] sts.
Row 9: {K1, p2, k1}, rep to end.
Row 10: P1, M1-p, work even in est rib patt until 1 st rem, M1-p, p1. 142 (146, 146, 146)[146, 150, 150, 154] sts.
Row 11: K1, {k1, p2, k1}, rep until 1 st rem, k1.
Row 12: P1, M1-p, work even in est rib patt until 1 st rem, M1-p, p1. 144 (148, 148, 148)[148, 152, 152, 156] sts.
Row 13: K2, {k1, p2, k1}, rep until 2 sts rem, k2.
Row 14: P1, M1L, p1, {p1, k1, M1L, k1, p1}, rep until 2 sts rem, p1, M1L, p1. 181 (186, 186, 186)[186, 191, 191, 196] sts.
Row 15: K1, p1, k1, {k1, p3, k1}, rep until 3 sts rem, k1, p1, k1.
Row 16: P1, M1L, work even in est rib patt until 1 st rem, M1L, p1. 183 (188, 188, 188)[188, 193, 193, 198] sts.

SHORT ROW SHAPING

Short Row 1 (RS): Work in even est rib patt until 4 sts rem, w&t.
Short Row 2 (WS): Work across row in est rib patt until 4 sts rem, w&t.
Short Row 3 (RS): Work in even est rib patt until 10 sts rem from last wrapped st, w&t.
Short Row 4 (WS): Work across row in est rib patt until 10 sts rem from last wrapped st, w&t.

Rep short rows 3 and 4, 6 times more. 35 (40, 40, 40)[40, 45, 45, 45, 50] sts between last wrapped sts.

Next row (RS): Work across row in est rib patt picking up and working wraps as you go.
Next row (WS): Work across row in est rib patt picking up and working wraps as you go.

BO all sts loosely in rib. Cut yarn.

Seam edges of collar down to top edges of buttonbands and BO edge of neck sts.

Set in sleeves and sew up side and arm seams.

Weave in all ends on the WS. Wet block to measurements. Sew on buttons opposite buttonholes.

☐	knit RS rows, purl WS rows	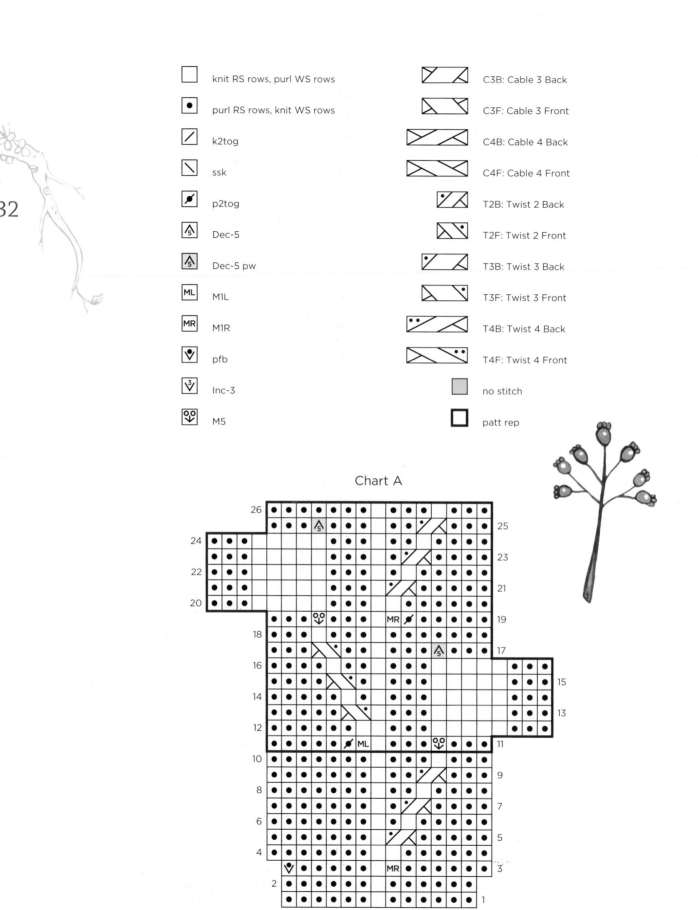 C3B: Cable 3 Back
•	purl RS rows, knit WS rows	C3F: Cable 3 Front
╱	k2tog	C4B: Cable 4 Back
╲	ssk	C4F: Cable 4 Front
◢	p2tog	T2B: Twist 2 Back
⟁₅	Dec-5	T2F: Twist 2 Front
⟁₅	Dec-5 pw	T3B: Twist 3 Back
ML	M1L	T3F: Twist 3 Front
MR	M1R	T4B: Twist 4 Back
⩔	pfb	T4F: Twist 4 Front
³⩔	Inc-3	no stitch
⩔⩔	M5	patt rep

Chart A

Chart B

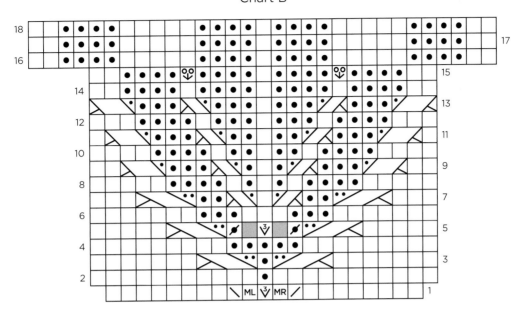

Chart C

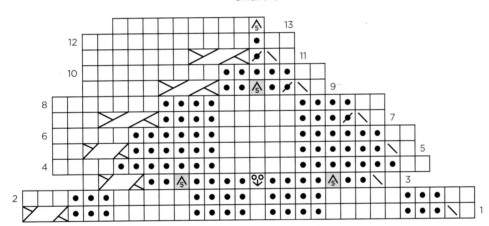

Chart D

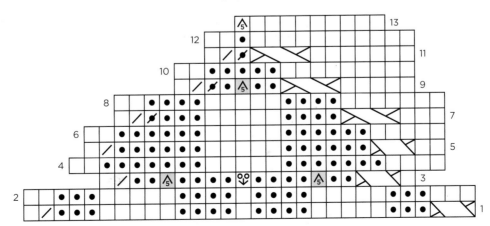

33

34

Chart A

Row 1 (RS): P6, k1, p6.

Row 2 (WS): K6, p1, k6.

Row 3: P6, M1R, k1, p5, pfb. 15 sts.

Row 4: K7, p2, k6.

Row 5: P5, T2B, k1, p7.

Row 6: K7, p1, k1, p1, k5.

Row 7: P4, T2B, p1, k1, p7.

Row 8: K7, p1, k2, p1, k4.

Row 9: P3, T2B, p2, k1, p7.

Row 10: K7, p1, k3, p1, k3.

Row 11: P3, M5, p3, k1, M1L, p2tog, p5. 19 sts.

Row 12: K6, p2, k3, p5, k3.

Row 13: P3, k5, p3, k1, T2F, p5.

Row 14: K5, p1, k1, p1, k3, p5, k3.

Row 15: P3, k5, p3, k1, p1, T2F, p4.

Row 16: K4, p1, k2, p1, k3, p5, k3.

Row 17: P3, Dec-5 pw, p3, k1, p2, T2F, p3. 15 sts.

Row 18: K3, p1, k3, p1, k7.

Row 19: P5, p2tog, M1R, k1, p3, M5, p3. 19 sts.

Row 20: K3, p5, k3, p2, k6.

Row 21: P5, T2B, k1, p3, k5, p3.

Row 22: K3, p5, k3, p1, k1, p1, k5.

Row 23: P4, T2B, p1, k1, p3, k5, p3.

Row 24: K3, p5, k3, p1, k2, p1, k4.

Row 25: P3, T2B, p2, k1, p3, Dec-5 pw, p3. 15 sts.

Row 26: K7, p1, k3, p1, k3.

Rep rows 11–26 for patt.

Chart B

Row 1 (RS): K8, k2tog, M1R, Inc-3, M1L, ssk, k8. 23 sts.

Row 2 (WS): P11, k1, p11.

Row 3: K7, T4B, p1, T4F, k7.

Row 4: P9, k5, p9.

Row 5: K5, T4B, p2tog, Inc-3, p2tog, T4F, k5.

Row 6: P7, k3, p3, k3, p7.

Row 7: K3, T4B, p2, T2B, k1, T2F, p2, T4F, k3.

Row 8: P5, k4, {p1, k1} twice, p1, k4, p5.

Row 9: K2, T3B, p3, T2B, p1, k1, p1, T2F, p3, T3F, k2.

Row 10: P4, k4, {p1, k2} twice, p1, k4, p4.

Row 11: K1, T3B, p3, T2B, p2, k1, p2, T2F, p3, T3F, k1.

Row 12: P3, k4, {p1, k3} twice, p1, k4, p3.

Row 13: T3B, p3, T2B, p3, k1, p3, T2F, p3, T3F.

Row 14: P2, {k4, p1} 3 times, k4, p2.

Row 15: K2, p4, M5, p4, k1, p4, M5, p4, k2. 31 sts.

Row 16: P2, k4, p5, k4, p1, k4, p5, k4, p2.

Row 17: K2, p4, k5, p4, k1, p4, k5, p4, k2.

Row 18: As for row 16.

Chart C

Row 1 (RS): K1, ssk, p3, k5, p4, k1, p4, k5, p3, C3B. 30 sts.

Row 2 (WS): P3, k3, p5, k4, p1, k4, p5, k3, p2.

Row 3: K1, ssk, p2, Dec-5 pw, p4, M5, p4, Dec-5 pw, p2, C3B, k1. 25 sts.

Row 4: P4, k7, p5, k7, p2.

Row 5: K1, ssk, p6, k5, p6, C3B, k2. 24 sts.

Row 6: {P5, k6} twice, p2.

Row 7: K1, ssk, p2tog, p3, k5, p4, C4B, k3. 22sts.

Row 8: P7, k4, p5, k4, p2.

Row 9: K1, ssk, p2tog, p1, Dec-5 pw, p2, C4B, k5. 16 sts.

Row 10: P9, k5, p2.

Row 11: K1, ssk, p2tog, C4B, k7. 14 sts.

Row 12: P11, k1, p2.

Row 13: Dec-5, k9. 10 sts.

Chart D

Row 1 (RS): C3F, p3, k5, p4, k1, p4, k5, p3, k2tog, k1. 30 sts.

Row 2 (WS): P2, k3, p5, k4, p1, k4, p5, k3, p3.

Row 3: K1, C3F, p2, Dec-5 pw, p4, M5, p4, Dec-5 pw, p2, k2tog, k1. 25 sts.

Row 4: P2, k7, p5, k7, p4.

Row 5: K2, C3F, p6, k5, p6, k2tog, k1. 24 sts.

Row 6: P2, {k6, p5} twice.

Row 7: K3, C4F, p4, k5, p3, p2tog, k2tog, k1. 22 sts.

Row 8: P2, k4, p5, k4, p7.

Row 9: K5, C4F, p2, Dec-5 pw, p1, p2tog, k2tog, k1. 16 sts.

Row 10: P2, k5, p9.

Row 11: K7, C4F, p2tog, k2tog, k1. 14 sts.

Row 12: P2, k1, p11.

Row 13: K9, Dec- 5. 10 sts.

twigs and willows

A classic and simple cardigan shape with two leafy branches
elegantly framing the neckline. *Twigs and Willows* is knit in pieces
from the bottom up and seamed together at the end.

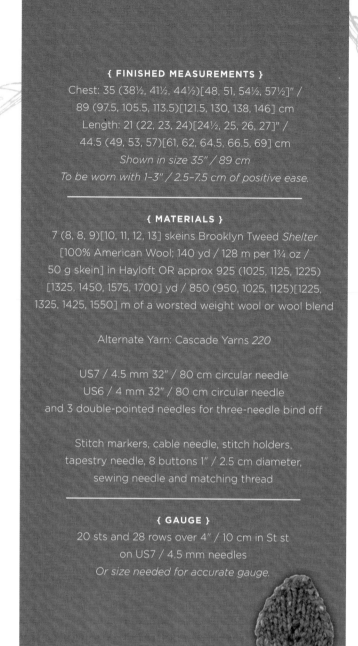

Back

CO 88 (96, 104, 112)[120, 128, 136, 144] sts onto larger circular needle.

Ribbing setup row (WS): P3, {k2, p2}, rep until 1 st rem, p1.

Work even in est rib patt until piece measures 1" / 2.5 cm from CO edge.

Dec row (RS): K2, ssk, work even in est rib patt until 4 sts rem, k2tog, k2. 2 sts dec.

Rep dec row every 4 rows 4 times more. 78 (86, 94, 102)[110, 118, 126, 134] sts.

Work even in est rib patt until piece measures 5" / 12.5 cm from CO edge. End with a WS row.

Knit 1 RS row.

Work even in St st for ½" / 1.5 cm. End with a WS row.

Inc row (RS): K3, M1R, knit until 3 sts rem, M1L, k3. 2 sts inc.

Rep inc row every 6 rows 4 times more. 88 (96, 104, 112)[120, 128, 136, 144] sts.

Work even in St st until piece measures 13½ (14, 14½, 15)[15, 15½, 16, 16½]" / 34.5 (35.5, 37, 38)[38, 39.5, 40.5, 42] cm from CO edge. End with a WS row.

ARMHOLE SHAPING

BO 5 (6, 7, 7)[8, 8, 9, 10] sts at beg of next 2 rows, then 0 (0, 0, 2)[3, 4, 5, 6] sts at beg of next 0 (0, 0, 2)[2, 2, 2, 2] rows.

Dec row (RS): K2, ssk, knit until 4 sts rem, k2tog, k2. 2 sts dec.

Rep dec row every RS row 2 (3, 4, 5)[6, 7, 8, 9] times more. 72 (76, 80, 82)[84, 88, 90, 92] sts.

Work even until armhole measures 7 (7½, 7¾, 8¼)[8½, 9, 9¼, 9¾]" / 18 (19, 19.5, 21)[21.5, 23, 23.5, 25] cm. End with a WS row.

SHOULDER SHAPING

Short Row 1 (RS): Knit until 6 (6, 6, 7)[7, 7, 8, 8] sts rem, w&t.
Short Row 2 (WS): Purl until 6 (6, 6, 7)[7, 7, 8, 8] sts rem, w&t.
Short Row 3 (RS): Knit until 6 (7, 7, 7)[8, 8, 8, 9] sts rem before last wrapped st, w&t.
Short Row 4 (WS): Purl until 6 (7, 7, 7)[8, 8, 8, 9] sts rem from last wrapped st, w&t.

Next row (RS): Knit across row picking up and knitting wraps as you go.
Next row (WS): Purl across row picking up and purling wraps as you go.
Next row (RS): K18 (19, 20, 21)[22, 23, 24, 25] shoulder sts, BO until 17 (18, 19, 20)[21, 22, 23, 24] sts rem, knit to end. Cut yarn. Slide unworked shoulder sts onto 2 separate stitch holders to be worked later. 18 (19, 20, 21)[22, 23, 24, 25] sts rem for each shoulder.

Left Front

CO 40 (44, 48, 52)[56, 60, 64, 68] sts onto larger circular needle.

Ribbing setup row (WS): P3, {k2, p2} rep until 1 st rem, p1.

Work even est rib patt until piece measures 1" / 2.5 cm from CO edge. End with a WS row.

Dec row (RS): K2, ssk, work even in est rib patt to end. 1 st dec.

Rep dec row every 4 rows 4 times more. 35 (39, 43, 47)[51, 55, 59, 63] sts.

Work even in est rib patt until piece measures 5" / 12.5 cm from CO edge. End with a WS row.

Knit 1 RS row.

38

Work even in St st for ½" / 1.5 cm. End with a WS row.

Inc row (RS): K3, M1R, knit to end. 1 st inc.

Rep inc row every 6 rows 4 times more. 40 (44, 48, 52)[56, 60, 64, 68] sts.

Work even in St st until piece measures 13½ (14, 14½, 15)[15, 15½, 16, 16½]" / 34.5 (35.5, 37, 38)[38, 39.5, 40.5, 42] cm from CO edge. End with a WS row.

ARMHOLE SHAPING
BO 5 (6, 7, 7)[8, 8, 9, 10] sts at beg of next row, then 0 (0, 0, 2)[3, 4, 5, 6] sts at beg of next 0 (0, 0, 1)[1, 1, 1, 1] RS row.

Purl 1 WS row.

Dec row (RS): K2, ssk, knit to end. 1 st dec.

Rep dec row every RS row 2 (3, 4, 5)[6, 7, 8, 9] times more.

AT THE SAME TIME, when armhole measures 1¼" / 3 cm, begin working chart patt as follows:

Next row (RS): Knit until 8 sts rem, pm, work Chart A over 8 sts.

Work rows 2–16 of Chart A, then work rows 13–16, 0 (0, 0, 0)[1, 1, 1, 1] time more, placing and moving markers as directed and working sts outside of chart as they appear. Work rows 17–25 of Chart A.

AT THE SAME TIME, after working row 19 of chart, work neckline shaping as follows:

Next row (WS): BO 9 sts, work even in est patt to end of row.
Dec row (RS): Work even in est patt until 3 sts rem, p2tog, k1. 1 st dec.

Rep dec row every RS row 4 (5, 6, 6)[6, 7, 7, 7] times more. 18 (19, 20, 21)[22, 23, 24, 25] sts.

Work even in est patt until armhole measures 7 (7½, 7¾, 8¼)[8½, 9, 9¼, 9¾]" / 18 (19, 19.5, 21)[21.5, 23, 23.5, 25] cm. End with a RS row.

SHOULDER SHAPING
Short Row 1 (WS): Work even in est patt until 6 (6, 6, 7)[7, 7, 8, 8] sts rem, w&t.
Short Row 2 (RS): Work to end.
Short Row 3 (WS): Work even in est patt until 6 (7, 7, 7)[8, 8, 8, 9] sts rem before last wrapped st, w&t.
Short Row 4 (RS): Work to end.

Next row (WS): Work across row in patt picking up and working wraps as you go. Remove markers.

Cut yarn. Slide shoulder sts onto a st holder to be worked later.

Right Front
CO 40 (44, 48, 52)[56, 60, 64, 68] sts onto larger circular needle.

Ribbing setup row (WS): P3, {k2, p2}, rep until 1 st rem, p1.

Work even in est rib patt until piece measures 1" / 2.5 cm from CO edge. End with a WS row.

Dec row (RS): Work even in est rib patt until 4 sts rem, k2tog, k2. 1 st dec.

Rep dec row every 4 rows 4 times more. 35 (39, 43, 47)[51, 55, 59, 63] sts.

Work even in est rib patt until piece measures 5" / 12.5 cm from CO edge. End with WS row.

Knit 1 RS row.

Work even in St st for ½" / 1.5 cm. End with a WS row.

Inc row (RS): Knit until 3 sts rem, M1L, k3. 1 st inc.

Rep inc row every 6 rows 4 times more. 40 (44, 48, 52)[56, 60, 64, 68] sts.

Work even in St st until piece measures 13½ (14, 14½, 15)[15, 15½, 16, 16½]" / 34.5 (35.5, 37, 38)[38, 39.5, 40.5, 42] cm from CO edge. End with a RS row.

ARMHOLE SHAPING
BO 5 (6, 7, 7)[8, 8, 9, 10] sts at beg of next row, then 0 (0, 0, 2)[3, 4, 5, 6] sts at beg of next 0 (0, 0, 1)[1, 1, 1, 1] WS row.

Dec row (RS): Knit until 4 sts rem, k2tog, k2. 1 st dec.

Rep dec row every RS row 2 (3, 4, 5)[6, 7, 8, 9] times more.

AT THE SAME TIME, when armhole measures 1¼" / 3 cm, beg working chart patt as follows:

Next row (RS): Work Chart B over 8 sts, pm, knit to end.

Work rows 2–16 of Chart B, then work rows 13–16 0 (0, 0, 0)[1, 1, 1, 1] time more, placing and moving markers as directed and working sts outside of chart as they appear. Work rows 17–25 of Chart B.

AT THE SAME TIME, after working row 20 of chart, work neckline shaping as follows:

Next row (RS): BO 9 sts, work even in est patt to end of row.

Work 1 WS row even.

Dec row (RS): K1, p2tog, work even in est patt to end of row. 1 st dec.

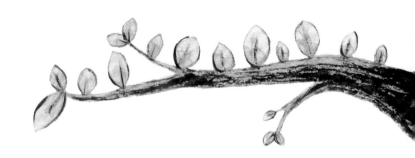

Rep dec row every RS row 4 (5, 6, 6)[6, 7, 7, 7] times more. 18 (19, 20, 21)[22, 23, 24, 25] sts.

Work even in patt until armhole measures 7 (7½, 7¾, 8¼)[8½, 9, 9¼, 9¾]" / 18 (19, 19.5, 21)[21.5, 23, 23.5, 25] cm. End with a WS row.

SHOULDER SHAPING

Short Row 1 (RS): Work even in est patt until 6 (6, 6, 7)[7, 7, 8, 8] sts rem, w&t.
Short Row 2 (WS): Work to end.
Short Row 3 (RS): Work even in est patt until 6 (7, 7, 7)[8, 8, 8, 9] sts rem before last wrapped st, w&t.
Short Row 4 (WS): Work to end.

Next row (RS): Work across row in patt picking up and working wraps as you go. Remove markers.

Cut yarn. Slide shoulder sts onto a st holder to be worked later.

Sleeves (MAKE 2)

CO 42 (42, 42, 42)[46, 46, 46, 46] sts onto larger circular needle.

Ribbing setup row (WS): P2, {k2, p2}, rep to end.

Work even in est rib patt until piece measures 2" / 5 cm from CO edge. End with a WS row.

Inc row (RS): K2, M1R, work until 3 sts rem, M1L, k2. 2 sts inc.

Working new sts into {k2, p2} rib as est, rep inc row every 14 (10, 8, 6)[6, 4, 4, 4] rows 4 (2, 3, 4)[8, 2, 14, 25] times more, then every 16 (12, 10, 8)[8, 6, 6, 0] rows 2 (6, 7, 9)[6, 15, 7, 0] times more. 56 (60, 64, 70)[76, 82, 90, 98] sts.

AT THE SAME TIME, when piece measures 5" / 12.5 cm from CO edge, beg working in St st.

Cont in St st until piece measures 17" / 43 cm from CO edge. End with a WS row.

SLEEVE CAP SHAPING

Next row (RS): BO 5 (6, 7, 7)[8, 8, 9, 10] sts at beg of next 2 rows, then 0 (0, 0, 2)[3, 4, 5, 6] sts at beg of next 0 (0, 0, 2)[2, 2, 2, 2] rows.

Dec row (RS): K2, ssk, knit until 4 sts rem, k2tog, k2. 2 sts dec.

Rep dec row every RS row 2 (3, 4, 5)[6, 7, 8, 9] times more, then every 4 rows 5 (6, 6, 6)[6, 6, 5, 5] times more, then every RS row 5 (4, 4, 4)[4, 5, 7, 8] times more. 20 sts.

Purl 1 WS row.

BO 2 sts at beg of next 2 rows, then 3 sts at beg of next 2 rows. BO rem 10 sts.

Finishing

Return shoulder sts to spare dpns and seam shoulders together using three-needle bind off method.

NECKBAND

With smaller circular needle and RS facing, beg at the right side of the neck opening and pick up and knit 32 (35, 36, 38)[38, 41, 41, 41] sts along right front, 36 (38, 40, 40)[40, 42, 42, 42] sts from back neck and 32 (35, 36, 38)[38, 41, 41, 41] sts along left front. 100 (108, 112, 116)[116, 124, 124, 124] sts.

Next row (WS): Knit all sts tbl.

Knit 3 rows. End with a RS row.

BO all sts.

BUTTON BAND

With smaller circular needle and RS facing, beg at the left front neck edge and pick up and knit 100 (100, 104, 108)[112, 116, 116, 120] sts along left front edge.

Ribbing setup row (WS): P3, {k2, p2}, rep until 1 st rem, p1.

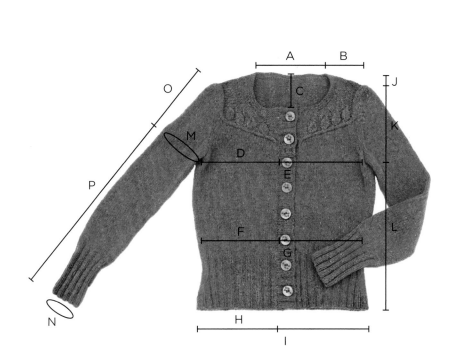

A	Back neck width	7¼ (7½, 8, 8)[8, 8½, 8½, 8½]" 18.5 (19.5, 20.5, 20.5)[20.5, 21.5, 21.5, 21.5] cm
B	Shoulder width	3½ (3¾, 4, 4¼)[4½, 4½, 4¾, 5]" 9 (9.5, 10, 10.5)[11, 11.5, 12, 12.5] cm
C	Neck depth	3¾ (4¼, 4½, 5)[4¾, 5¼, 5½, 6]" 9.5 (11, 11.5, 12.5)[12, 13, 14, 15] cm
D, H	Front width (chest/hip)	8 (8¾, 9½, 10½)[11¼, 12, 12¾, 13½]" 20.5 (22.5, 24.5, 26.5)[28.5, 30.5, 32.5, 34.5] cm
E, I	Back width (chest/hip)	17½ (19¼, 20¾, 22½)[24, 25½, 27¼, 28¾]" 44.5 (49, 53, 57)[61, 65, 69, 73] cm
F	Front width (waist)	7 (7¾, 8½, 9½)[10¼, 11, 11¾, 12½]" 18 (20, 22, 24)[26, 28, 30, 32] cm
G	Back width (waist)	15½ (17¼, 18¾, 20½)[22, 23½, 25¼, 26¾]" 39.5 (43.5, 48, 52)[56, 60, 64, 68] cm
J	Shoulder height	½" / 1.5 cm
K	Armhole depth	7¼ (7¾, 8, 8½)[8¾, 9¼, 9½, 10]" 18.5 (20, 20.5, 21.5)[22.5, 23.5, 24, 25.5] cm
L	Side length	13½ (14, 14½, 15)[15, 15½, 16, 16½]" 34.5 (35.5, 37, 38)[38, 39.5, 40.5, 42] cm
M	Upper arm circ	11¼ (12, 12¾, 14)[15¼, 16½, 18, 19½]" 28.5 (30.5, 32.5, 35.5)[38.5, 41.5, 45.5, 50] cm
N	Cuff circ	8½ (8½, 8½, 8½)[9¼, 9¼, 9¼, 9¼]" 21.5 (21.5, 21.5, 21.5)[23.5, 23.5, 23.5, 23.5] cm
O	Cap height	5¾ (6¼, 6½, 6¾)[7¼, 7¾, 8, 8½]" 14.5 (16, 16.5, 17.5)[18, 19.5, 20.5, 22] cm
P	Sleeve length	17" / 43 cm

Cont in est rib patt for 10 rows more. End with a WS row.

Next row (RS): BO all sts in rib.

BUTTONHOLE BAND

With smaller needle and RS facing, beg at the bottom CO edge of right front and pick up and knit 100 (100, 104, 108)[112, 116, 116, 120] sts along right front edge.

Ribbing setup row (WS): P3, {k2, p2}, rep, until 1 st rem, p1.

Cont in est rib patt for 4 rows more. End with a WS row.

Buttonhole row (RS): {Work 9 (9, 9, 10)[9, 9, 9, 10] sts in patt, BO 2, work 9 (9, 10, 10)[9, 10, 10, 10] sts in patt, BO 2}, 4 times total,

then {work 0 (0, 0, 0)[9, 9, 9, 9] sts in patt, BO 2} 0 (0, 0, 0)[1, 1, 1, 1] time(s) total, p1, k3.

Next row (WS): Work across row in est rib patt. Using backwards loop method, CO 2 sts over each BO space.

Cont in est rib patt for 4 rows more. End with a WS row.

BO all sts in rib.

Set in sleeves and sew up side and arm seams. Weave in all ends on the WS. Wet block to measurements. Sew on buttons opposite buttonholes.

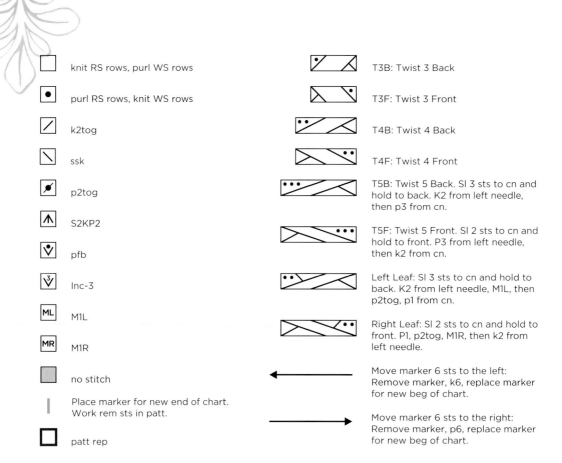

knit RS rows, purl WS rows

purl RS rows, knit WS rows

k2tog

ssk

p2tog

S2KP2

pfb

Inc-3

ML — M1L

MR — M1R

no stitch

Place marker for new end of chart. Work rem sts in patt.

patt rep

T3B: Twist 3 Back

T3F: Twist 3 Front

T4B: Twist 4 Back

T4F: Twist 4 Front

T5B: Twist 5 Back. Sl 3 sts to cn and hold to back. K2 from left needle, then p3 from cn.

T5F: Twist 5 Front. Sl 2 sts to cn and hold to front. P3 from left needle, then k2 from cn.

Left Leaf: Sl 3 sts to cn and hold to back. K2 from left needle, M1L, then p2tog, p1 from cn.

Right Leaf: Sl 2 sts to cn and hold to front. P1, p2tog, M1R, then k2 from left needle.

Move marker 6 sts to the left: Remove marker, k6, replace marker for new beg of chart.

Move marker 6 sts to the right: Remove marker, p6, replace marker for new beg of chart.

44

Chart A

Row 1 (RS): K3, T4B, k1.
Row 2 (WS): P1, k2, p5.
Row 3: Make Left Leaf, p2, k1.
Row 4: P1, k4, p3, remove marker, p6, pm. 14 sts.
Row 5: K3, T5B, Inc-3, p4, k1. 16 sts.
Row 6: P1, k4, p1, k1, p1, k3, p5.
Row 7: Make Left Leaf, p2, k2tog, M1R, p1, M1L, k1, pfb, pm for end of chart, work former chart sts in patt to end of row. 14 sts.
Row 8: K2, p2, k1, p2, k4, p3, remove marker, p6, pm. 20 sts.
Row 9: K3, T5B, Inc-3, p3, k2tog, k1, p1, k2, pfb, p1. 22 sts.
Row 10: K3, p5, k3, p1, k1, p1, k3, p5.
Row 11: Make Left Leaf, p2, k2tog, M1R, p1, M1L, k1, pfb, p2, ssk, k1, k2tog, p3.
Row 12: K3, p3, k4, p2, k1, p2, k4, p3, remove marker, p6, pm. 28 sts.
Row 13: K3, T5B, Inc-3, p3, k2tog, k1, p1, k2, pfb, p3, S2KP2, p3.
Row 14: K9, p5, k3, p1, k1, p1, k3, p5.
Row 15: Make Left Leaf, p2, k2tog, M1R, p1, M1L, k1, pfb, p2, ssk, k1, k2tog, p3, pm for end of chart, work former chart sts in patt. 22 sts.
Row 16: K3, p3, k4, p2, k1, p2, k4, p3, remove marker, p6, pm. 28 sts.
Row 17: K4, T4B, Inc-3, p3, k2tog, k1, p1, k2, pfb, p3, S2KP2, p3.
Row 18: K9, p5, k3, p1, k1, p1, k2, p6.
Row 19: K3, T3B, p2, k1, M1R, p1, M1L, k1, p3, ssk, k1, k2tog, p3, pm for end of chart, work former chart sts in patt. 22 sts.
Row 20: K3, p3, k3, p2, k1, p2, k3, p5.
Row 21: K2, T3B, p3, k2, p1, k2, p3, S2KP2, p3. 20 sts.
Row 22: K7, p5, k4, p4.
Row 23: K4, p4, ssk, k1, k2tog, p1, pm for end of chart, work former chart sts in patt. 12 sts.
Row 24: K1, p3, k4, p4.
Row 25: K4, p4, S2KP2, p1. 10 sts.

Chart B

Row 1 (RS): K1, T4F, k3.
Row 2 (WS): P5, k2, p1.
Row 3: K1, p2, make Right Leaf, remove marker, k6, pm. 14 sts.
Row 4: P9, k4, p1.
Row 5: K1, p4, Inc-3, T5F, k3. 16 sts.
Row 6: P5, k3, p1, k1, p1, k4, p1.
Row 7: K1, p3, pm for new beg of chart, pfb, k1, M1R, p1, M1L, ssk, p2, make Right Leaf, remove marker, k6, pm. 20 sts.
Row 8: P9, k4, p2, k1, p2, k2.
Row 9: P1, pfb, k2, p1, k1, ssk, p3, Inc-3, T5F, k3. 22 sts.
Row 10: P5, k3, p1, k1, p1, k3, p5, k3.
Row 11: P3, ssk, k1, k2tog, p2, pfb, k1, M1R, p1, M1L, ssk, p2, make Right Leaf, remove marker, k6, pm. 28 sts.
Row 12: P9, k4, p2, k1, p2, k4, p3, k3.
Row 13: P3, S2KP2, p3, pfb, k2, p1, k1, ssk, p3, Inc-3, T5F, k3.
Row 14: P5, k3, p1, k1, p1, k3, p5, k9.
Row 15: Remove marker, p6, pm for new beg of chart, p3, ssk, k1, k2tog, p2, pfb, k1, M1R, p1, M1L, ssk, p2, make Right Leaf, remove marker, k6, pm.
Row 16: P9, k4, p2, k1, p2, k4, p3, k3.
Row 17: P3, S2KP2, p3, pfb, k2, p1, k1, ssk, p3, Inc-3, T4F, k4.
Row 18: P6, k2, p1, k1, p1, k3, p5, k9.
Row 19: Remove marker, p6, pm for new beg of chart, p3, ssk, k1, k2tog, p3, k1, M1R, p1, M1L, k1, p2, T3F, k3. 22 sts.
Row 20: P5, k3, p2, k1, p2, k3, p3, k3.
Row 21: P3, S2KP2, p3, k2, p1, k2 p3, T3F, k2. 20 sts.
Row 22: P4, k4, p5, k7.
Row 23: Remove marker, p6, pm for new beg of chart, p1, ssk, k1, k2tog, p4, k4. 12 sts.
Row 24: P4, k4, p3, k1.
Row 25: P1, S2KP2, p4, k4. 10 sts.

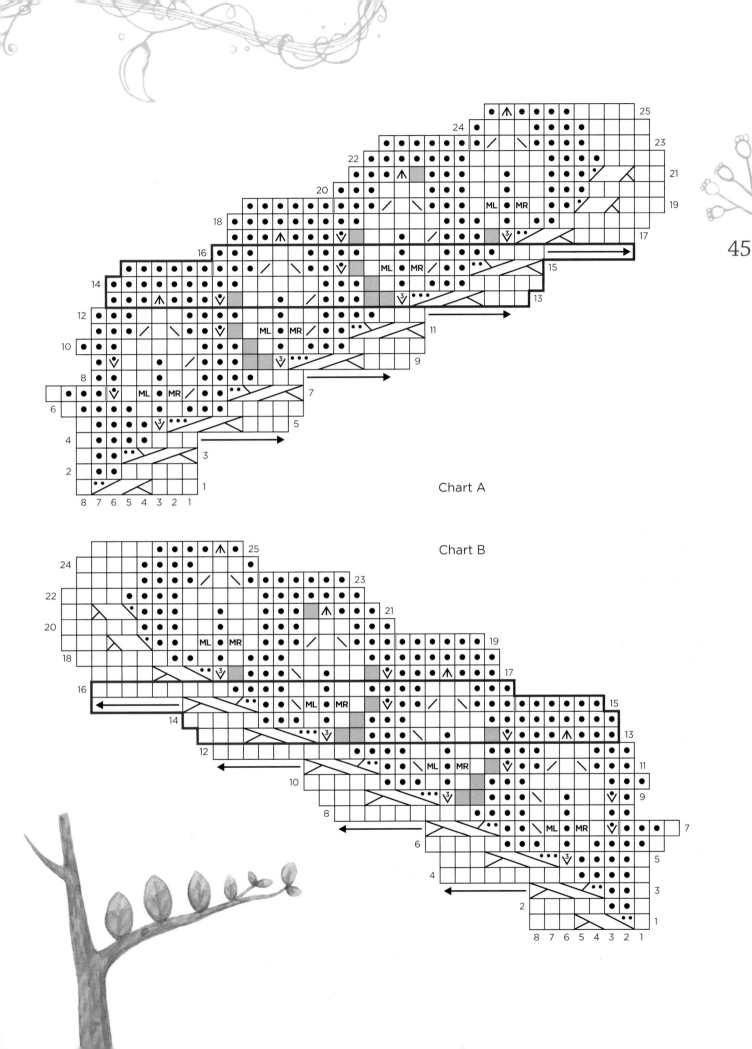

Chart A

Chart B

entangled vines

This top down raglan cardigan features a lovely entangled cable and leaf design cascading down the sleeves. Knit in one piece with worsted weight yarn, this cardigan knits up quickly and keeps your interest.

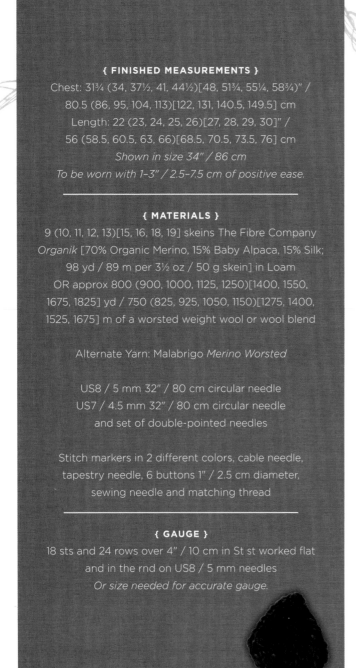

{ FINISHED MEASUREMENTS }

Chest: 31¾ (34, 37½, 41, 44½)[48, 51¾, 55¼, 58¾)" /
80.5 (86, 95, 104, 113)[122, 131, 140.5, 149.5] cm
Length: 22 (23, 24, 25, 26)[27, 28, 29, 30]" /
56 (58.5, 60.5, 63, 66)[68.5, 70.5, 73.5, 76] cm
Shown in size 34" / 86 cm
To be worn with 1–3" / 2.5–7.5 cm of positive ease.

{ MATERIALS }

9 (10, 11, 12, 13)[15, 16, 18, 19] skeins The Fibre Company
Organik [70% Organic Merino, 15% Baby Alpaca, 15% Silk;
98 yd / 89 m per 3½ oz / 50 g skein] in Loam
OR approx 800 (900, 1000, 1125, 1250)[1400, 1550,
1675, 1825] yd / 750 (825, 925, 1050, 1150)[1275, 1400,
1525, 1675] m of a worsted weight wool or wool blend

Alternate Yarn: Malabrigo *Merino Worsted*

US8 / 5 mm 32" / 80 cm circular needle
US7 / 4.5 mm 32" / 80 cm circular needle
and set of double-pointed needles

Stitch markers in 2 different colors, cable needle,
tapestry needle, 6 buttons 1" / 2.5 cm diameter,
sewing needle and matching thread

{ GAUGE }

18 sts and 24 rows over 4" / 10 cm in St st worked flat
and in the rnd on US8 / 5 mm needles
Or size needed for accurate gauge.

Yoke

CO 60 (60, 62, 64, 66)[68, 70, 72, 74] sts onto larger circular needle. Do not join into the rnd.

Setup row (WS): P3 left front sts, pm, p9 sleeve sts, pm, p36 (36, 38, 40, 42)[44, 46, 48, 50] back sts, pm, p9 sleeve sts, pm, p3 right front sts.

Working in St st, beg raglan inc and establish chart patt over sleeve sts as follows:

Inc row (RS): K1, M1R, {knit to 1 st before marker, M1R, k1, sm, k1, M1R, work chart, M1L, k1, sm, k1, M1L}, rep once more, knit until 1 st rem, M1L, k1. 10 sts inc.

NOTE: Chart is worked over center sleeve sts, incorporating new sts created by raglan inc into chart patt until there are 23 sts worked in chart patt, then rem sleeve sts are worked in St st.

Rep inc row every RS row 3 (4, 4, 4, 5)[5, 5, 6, 6] times more. 100 (110, 112, 114, 126)[128, 130, 142, 144] sts: 11 (13, 13, 13, 15)[15, 15, 17, 17] front sts, 17 (19, 19, 19, 21)[21, 21, 23, 23] sleeve sts, 44 (46, 48, 50, 54)[56, 58, 62, 64] back sts.

Work 1 WS row.

Next row (RS): {Knit to 1 st before marker, M1R, k1, sm, k1, M1R, work to 1 st before marker, M1L, k1, sm, k1, M1L}, rep once more, knit to end. Using backwards loop cast on method, CO 8 (8, 9, 10, 10)[11, 12, 12, 13] sts.

Next row (WS): Work even to end of row, then using backwards loop cast on method, CO 8 (8, 9, 10, 10)[11, 12, 12, 13] sts. 124 (134, 138, 142, 154)[158, 162, 174, 178] sts: 20 (22, 23, 24, 26)[27, 28, 30, 31] front sts, 19 (21, 21, 21, 23)[23, 23, 25, 25] sleeve sts, 46 (48, 50, 52, 56)[58, 60, 64, 66] back sts.

NOTE: When there are 25 sleeve sts total, place markers according to chart directions and work 23 center sts in chart patt as est and rem sleeve sts on either side in St st.

Inc row: {Knit to 1 st before marker, M1R, k1, sm, k1, M1R, work to 1 st before marker, M1L, k1, sm, k1, M1L}, rep once more, knit to end. 8 sts inc.

Rep inc row every RS row 9 (10, 12, 14, 15)[17, 19, 20, 22] times more. 204 (222, 242, 262, 282)[302, 322, 342, 362] sts: 30 (33, 36, 39, 42)[45, 48, 51, 54] front sts, 39 (43, 47, 51, 55)[59, 63, 67, 71] sleeve sts, 66 (70, 76, 82, 88)[94, 100, 106, 112] back sts.

Cont as est, working even in St st over fronts and back sections and the chart patt over sleeves, for 5 rows more. End on chart row 34 (38, 42, 46, 50)[54, 58, 62, 66] for sleeves. Yoke measures approx 5¾ (6½, 7¼, 7¾, 8½)[9¼, 9¾, 10½, 11¼]" / 15 (16.5, 18, 20, 21.5)[23.5, 25, 26.5, 28.5] cm.

DIVIDE FOR SLEEVES

Next row (RS): {Knit to marker, slide 39 (43, 47, 51, 55)[59, 63, 67, 71] sleeve sts on a holder, removing markers. Using backwards loop cast on method, CO 3 (3, 4, 5, 6)[7, 8, 9, 10] sts, pm, CO 3 (3, 4, 5, 6)[7, 8, 9, 10] sts}, rep once more, knit to end. 138 (148, 164, 180, 196)[212, 228, 244, 260] sts: 33 (36, 40, 44, 48)[52, 56, 60, 64] front sts, 72 (76, 84, 92, 100)[108, 116, 124, 132] back sts.

Work even in St st until work measures 7½" / 19 cm from underarm. End with a WS row.

Inc row (RS): {Knit to 1 st before marker, M1R, k1, sm, k1, M1L}, rep once more, knit to end. 142 (152, 168, 184, 200)[216, 232, 248, 264] sts.

Work even in St st until work measures 14¼ (14½, 15, 15¼, 15½)[16, 16¼, 16½, 17]" / 36 (37, 38, 38.5, 39.5)[40.5, 41.5, 42, 43] cm from underarm. End with a RS row.

Knit 8 rows. Remove markers.

BO all sts knitwise.

Sleeves (MAKE 2)

Divide 39 (43, 47, 51, 55)[59, 63, 67, 71] held sts evenly among dpns. Pick up and knit 8 (8, 10, 12, 14)[16, 18, 20, 22] sts from CO at underarm, pm in the middle of the picked up sts to mark beg of rnd. 47 (51, 57, 63, 69)[75, 81, 87, 93] sts.

Rnd 1: Work sts as est, beg with chart row 35 (39, 43, 47, 51)[55, 59, 63, 67] over marked center sts, until 5 (5, 6, 7, 8)[9, 10, 11, 12] sts rem, ssk, k3 (3, 4, 5, 6)[7, 8, 9, 10].
Rnd 2: K3 (3, 4, 5, 6)[7, 8, 9, 10], k2tog, work even as est. 45 (49, 55, 61, 67)[73, 79, 85, 91] sts.

Cont in est patt for 25 (19, 12, 7, 5)[4, 3, 2, 2] rnds more.

Dec rnd: K1, ssk, work until 3 sts rem, k2tog, k1. 2 sts dec.

Rep dec rnd every 0 (21, 14, 9, 7)[6, 5, 4, 4] rnds 0 (1, 1, 5, 5)[3, 5, 12, 6] time(s) more, then every 0 (0, 13, 0, 6)[5, 4, 3, 3] rnds 0 (0, 2, 0, 2)[6, 6, 1, 9] time(s) more. 43 (45, 47, 49, 51)[53, 55, 57, 59] sts.

Work even until sleeve measures 10" / 25.5 cm from underarm.

Rnd 1: Purl.
Rnd 2: Knit.

Rep last 2 rnds 3 times more. Remove markers.

BO all sts purlwise.

Rep for second sleeve.

Finishing
NECKBAND

With smaller circular needle and RS facing, beg at CO sts for right front neck, pick up and knit 8 (8, 9, 10, 10)[11, 12, 12, 13] sts along CO edge, 10 (10, 10, 10, 11)[11, 11, 12, 12] sts along side neck to original CO sts, 58 (58, 60, 62, 64)[66, 68, 70, 72] sts along CO edge, 10 (10, 10, 10, 11)[11, 11, 12, 12] sts along side neck, and 8 (8, 9, 10, 10)[11, 12, 12, 13] sts along left front edge to hem. 94 (94, 98, 102, 106)[110, 114, 118, 122] sts.

Knit 6 rows. End with a RS row.

BO all sts knitwise.

BUTTON BAND

With smaller circular needle and RS facing, beg at the neck edge, pick up and knit 88 (90, 94, 98, 102)[106, 110, 114, 118] sts along left front edge.

Knit 8 rows. End with a RS row.

BO all sts knitwise.

BUTTONHOLE BAND

With smaller circular needle and RS facing, beg at the bottom CO edge, pick up and knit 88 (90, 94, 98, 102)[106, 110, 114, 118] sts along right front edge.

Knit 3 rows. End with a WS row.

Buttonhole row (RS): K4, {BO 3, k11 (12, 12, 10, 11)[12, 12, 10, 11] sts} 2 (4, 1, 2, 4)[5, 2, 1, 4] time(s) total, {BO 3, k12 (12, 13, 11, 12) [12, 13, 11, 12] sts} 3 (1, 4, 4, 2)[1, 4, 6, 3] time(s) total, BO 3, k2.
Next row (WS): Knit across row. Using backwards loop cast on method, CO 3 sts over each BO space.

Knit 3 rows. End with a RS row.

BO all sts knitwise.

Sew on buttons opposite buttonholes. Weave in all ends on the WS. Wet block to measurements.

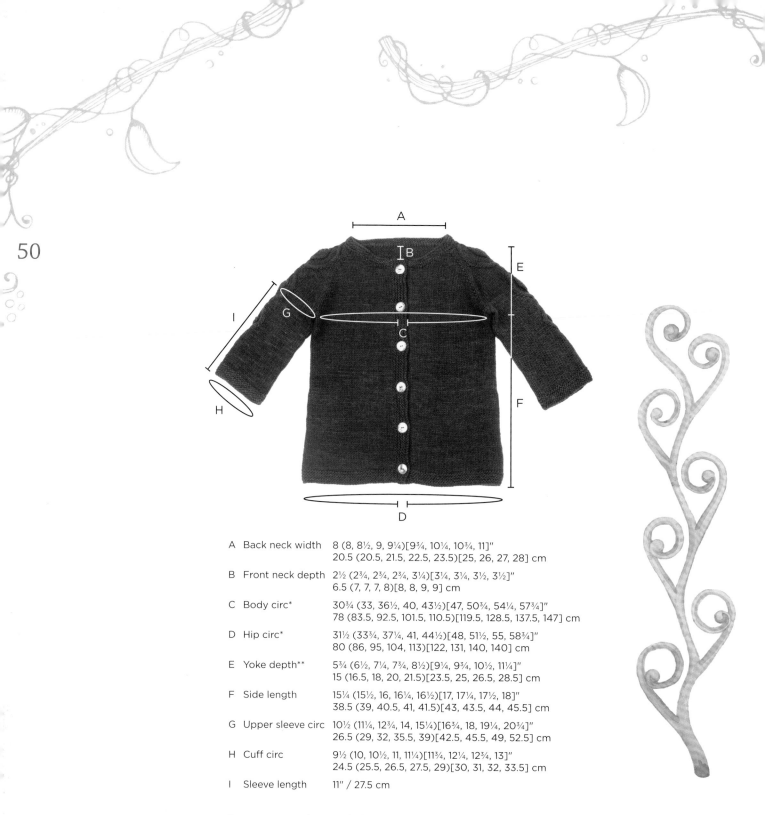

A	Back neck width	8 (8, 8½, 9, 9¼)[9¾, 10¼, 10¾, 11]" 20.5 (20.5, 21.5, 22.5, 23.5)[25, 26, 27, 28] cm
B	Front neck depth	2½ (2¾, 2¾, 2¾, 3¼)[3¼, 3¼, 3½, 3½]" 6.5 (7, 7, 7, 8)[8, 8, 9, 9] cm
C	Body circ*	30¾ (33, 36½, 40, 43½)[47, 50¾, 54¼, 57¾]" 78 (83.5, 92.5, 101.5, 110.5)[119.5, 128.5, 137.5, 147] cm
D	Hip circ*	31½ (33¾, 37¼, 41, 44½)[48, 51½, 55, 58¾]" 80 (86, 95, 104, 113)[122, 131, 140, 140] cm
E	Yoke depth**	5¾ (6½, 7¼, 7¾, 8½)[9¼, 9¾, 10½, 11¼]" 15 (16.5, 18, 20, 21.5)[23.5, 25, 26.5, 28.5] cm
F	Side length	15¼ (15½, 16, 16¼, 16½)[17, 17¼, 17½, 18]" 38.5 (39, 40.5, 41, 41.5)[43, 43.5, 44, 45.5] cm
G	Upper sleeve circ	10½ (11¼, 12¾, 14, 15¼)[16¾, 18, 19¼, 20¾]" 26.5 (29, 32, 35.5, 39)[42.5, 45.5, 49, 52.5] cm
H	Cuff circ	9½ (10, 10½, 11, 11¼)[11¾, 12¼, 12¾, 13]" 24.5 (25.5, 26.5, 27.5, 29)[30, 31, 32, 33.5] cm
I	Sleeve length	11" / 27.5 cm

* measurement does not include button band

** measurement does not include neckband

Chart

Row 1 (RS): Knit.

Row 2 (WS): Purl.

Row 3: K2, C5F, k2. 9 sts.

Row 4: Purl.

Row 5: K1, T4B, k1, T4F, k1. 11 sts.

Row 6: P3, k2, p1, k2, p3.

Row 7: T4B, p2, k1, p2, T4F. 13 sts.

Row 8: P2, k4, p1, k4, p2.

Row 9: K2tog, k1, p4, Inc-3, p4, k1, ssk. 15 sts.

Row 10: P2, k4, p3, k4, p2.

Row 11: K2tog, k1, p4, {k1, yo} twice, k1, p4, k1, ssk. 17 sts.

Row 12: P2, k4, p5, k4, p2.

Row 13: K2tog, k1, p4, k2, yo, k1, yo, k2, p4, k1, ssk. 19 sts.

Row 14: P2, k4, p7, k4, p2.

Row 15: K2tog, k1, p4, k3, yo, k1, yo, k3, p4, k1, ssk. 21 sts.

Row 16: P2, k4, p9, k4, p2.

Row 17: Pm, k1, M1R, k2, p4, ssk, k5, k2tog, p4, k2, M1L, k1, pm. 23 sts.

Row 18: P4, k4, p7, k4, p4.

Row 19: K2, M1R, k2, p4, ssk, k3, k2tog, p4, k2, M1L, k2.

Row 20: {P5, k4} twice, p5.

Row 21: K3, M1R, k2, p4, ssk, k1, k2tog, p4, k2, M1L, k3.

Row 22: P6, k4, p3, k4, p6.

Row 23: K4, M1R, k2, p4, S2KP2, p4, k2, M1L, k4.

Row 24: P7, k9, p7.

Row 25: K5, C4F, p5, C4B, k5.

Row 26: P9, k5, p9.

Row 27: K7, C4F, p1, C4B, k7.

Row 28: P11, k1, p11.

Row 29: K9, C5F, k9.

Row 30: Purl.

Row 31: Knit.

Row 32: Purl.

Row 33: As for row 29.

Row 34: Purl.

Row 35: K7, T4B, k1, T4F, k7.

Row 36: P9, k2, p1, k2, p9.

Row 37: K6, T3B, p2, k1, p2, T3F, k6.

Row 38: P8, k3, p1, k3, p8.

Row 39: K5, k2tog, k1, p3, Inc-3, p3, k1, ssk, k5.

Row 40: P7, k3, p3, k3, p7.

Row 41: K4, k2tog, k1, p3, {k1, yo} twice, k1, p3, k1, ssk, k4.

Row 42: P6, k3, p5, k3, p6.

Row 43: K3, k2tog, k1, p3, k2, yo, k1, yo, k2, p3, k1, ssk, k3.

Row 44: P5, k3, p7, k3, p5.

Row 45: K3, M1R, k2, p3, ssk, k3, k2tog, p3, k2, M1L, k3.

Row 46: As for row 42.

Row 47: K4, M1R, k2, p3, ssk, k1, k2tog, p3, k2, M1L, k4.

Row 48: As for row 40.

Row 49: K5, M1R, k2, p3, S2KP2, p3, k2, M1L, k5.

Row 50: P8, k7, p8.

Row 51: K6, C3F, p5, C3B, k6.

Row 52: P9, k5, p9.

Row 53: K7, C4F, p1, C4B, k7.

Row 54: P11, k1, p11.

Row 55: K9, C5F, k9.

Row 56: Purl.

Row 57: Knit.

Row 58: Purl.

Row 59: As for row 55.

Row 60: Purl.

Row 61: K8, T3B, k1, T3F, k8.

Row 62: P10, k1, p1, k1, p10.

Row 63: K7, T3B, p1, k1, p1, T3F, k7.

Row 64: P9, k2, p1, k2, p9.

Row 65: K6, k2tog, k1, p2, Inc-3, p2, k1, ssk, k6.

Row 66: P8, k2, p3, k2, p8.

Row 67: K5, k2tog, k1, p2, {k1, yo} twice, k1, p2, k1, ssk, k5.

Row 68: P7, k2, p5, k2, p7.

Row 69: K5, M1R, k2, p2, ssk, k1, k2tog, p2, k2, M1L, k5.

Row 70: As for row 66.

Row 71: K6, M1R, k2, p2, S2KP2, p2, k2, M1L, k6.

Row 72: P9, k5, p9.

Row 73: K7, C3F, p3, C3B, k7.

Row 74: P10, k3, p10.

Row 75: K8, C3F, p1, C3B, k8.

Row 76: P11, k1, p11.

Row 77: K9, C5F, k9.

Chart

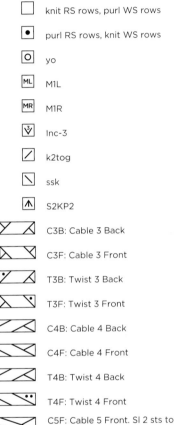

- ☐ knit RS rows, purl WS rows
- • purl RS rows, knit WS rows
- Ⓞ yo
- ML M1L
- MR M1R
- ⅴ Inc-3
- ╱ k2tog
- ╲ ssk
- ⋀ S2KP2
- ▱ C3B: Cable 3 Back
- ▱ C3F: Cable 3 Front
- ▱ T3B: Twist 3 Back
- ▱ T3F: Twist 3 Front
- ▱ C4B: Cable 4 Back
- ▱ C4F: Cable 4 Front
- ▱ T4B: Twist 4 Back
- ▱ T4F: Twist 4 Front
- ▱ C5F: Cable 5 Front. Sl 2 sts to cn and hold to front, k3, then k2 from cn.
- | place marker
- ▨ no stitch

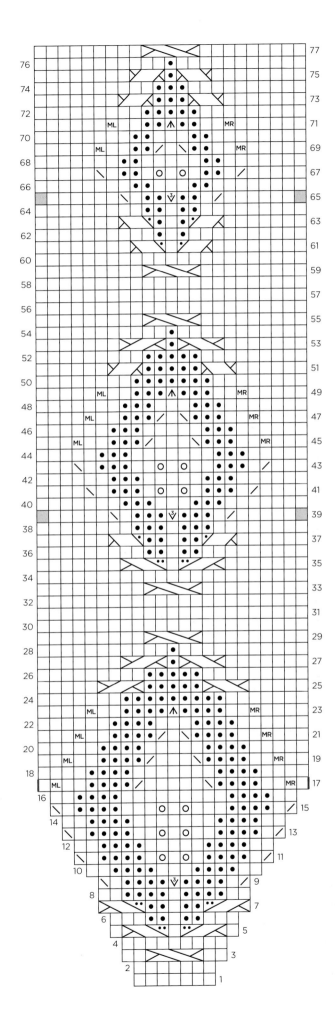

53

ACCESSORIES

forest floor

A slouchy style hat featuring a subtle layered leaf stitch pattern
reminiscent of the fallen leaves of autumn. Warm, cozy
and the perfect accessory for cooler weather.

{ SIZE }
Stretches to fit a 20–22" / 51–56 cm head circ

{ FINISHED MEASUREMENTS }
Brim circ: 18" / 46 cm unstretched

{ MATERIALS }
1 skein Blue Sky Alpacas *Suri Merino*
[60% Baby Suri, 40% Merino; 164 yd / 150 m
per 3½ oz / 100g skein] in Harvest OR approx 150 yd /
140 m of a dk weight wool or wool blend

Alternate Yarn: Berroco *Ultra Alpaca*

US5 / 3.75 mm 16" / 40 cm circular needle
US7 / 4.5 mm 16" / 40 cm circular needle
and set of double-pointed needles

Stitch marker, cable needle, tapestry needle

{ GAUGE }
20 sts and 28 rows over 4" / 10 cm in St st
worked in the rnd on US7 / 4.5 mm needles
Or size needed for accurate gauge.

Brim

CO 120 sts onto smaller circular needle. Pm, join for working in the rnd being careful not to twist your sts.

Ribbing setup rnd: {K1, p2}, rep to end.

Work even in est rib patt for 1" / 2.5 cm.

Switch to larger circular needle.

Knit 2 rnds.

Work rnds 1–48 of chart patt. Switch to dpns when work becomes too tight on the circular needle.

Next rnd: Move marker 1 st to the left, k2tog 7 times total, k1. 8 sts.

Next rnd: K2tog 4 times total. 4 sts. Remove marker.

Finishing

Cut yarn, thread tail onto tapestry needle, pass through rem sts and cinch to close.

Weave in all ends on the WS.

Wet block.

Chart (WORKED 5 TIMES AROUND)

Rnd 1: {K4, k2tog, yo, k1, yo, ssk, k9, p1, k5}, rep.

Rnd 2: {K18, p1, k5}, rep.

Rnd 3: {K2, C4B, p1, C4F, k2, C4B, k1, M1R, p1, M1L, k1, C4F}, rep. 130 sts.

Rnd 4: {K6, p1, k19}, rep.

Rnd 5: {K6, p1, k11, S2KP2, k5}, rep. 120 sts.

Rnd 6: {K6, p1, k17}, rep.

Rnd 7: {C4B, k2, p1, k2, C4F, k2, yo, k2, S2KP2, k2, yo, k2}, rep.

Rnd 8: As for rnd 6.

Rnd 9: {K6, p1, k9, yo, k1, S2KP2, k1, yo, k3}, rep.

Rnd 10: As for rnd 6.

Rnd 11: {C4B, k2, p1, k2, C4F, k4, yo, S2KP2, yo, k4}, rep.

Rnd 12: As for rnd 6.

Rnd 13: {K6, p1, k9, k2tog, yo, k1, yo, ssk, k3}, rep.

Rnd 14: As for rnd 6.

Rnd 15: {K1, C4B, k1, M1R, p1, M1L, k1, C4F, k2, C4B, p1, C4F, k1}, rep. 130 sts.

Rnd 16: {K20, p1, k5}, rep.

Rnd 17: {K6, S2KP2, k11, p1, k5}, rep. 120 sts.

Rnd 18: As for rnd 2.

Rnd 19: Move marker 1 st to the left: remove marker, sl 1 st from left needle to right needle, replace marker for new beg of rnd. {K2, yo, k2, S2KP2, k2, yo, k2, C4B, k2, p1, k2, C4F}, rep.

Rnd 20: {K17, p1, k6}, rep.

Rnd 21: {K3, yo, k1, S2KP2, k1, yo, k9, p1, k6}, rep.

Rnd 22: As for rnd 20.

Rnd 23: {K4, yo, S2KP2, yo, k4, C4B, k2, p1, k2, C4F}, rep.

Rnd 24: {K17, p1, k6}, rep until 1 st rem. Move marker 1 st to the right: sl 1 st from left needle to right needle, remove marker, sl 1 st back to left needle, replace marker for new beg of rnd.

Rnds 25-34: As for rnds 1–10.

Rnd 35: {C4B, k2, p1, k2, C4F, k4, yo, S2KP2, yo, k4}, rep until 1 st rem. Move marker 1 st to the right.

Rnd 36: {K2tog, k5, p1, k5, ssk, k9}, rep until 1 st rem. Move marker 1 st to the right. 110 sts.

Rnd 37: {K2tog, k5, p1, k5, ssk, k7}, rep until 1 st rem. Move marker 1 st to the right. 100 sts.

Rnd 38: {K2tog, k5, p1, k5, ssk, k5}, rep. 90 sts.

Rnd 39: {K1, C4B, k1, M1R, p1, M1L, k1, C4F, k6}, rep. 100 sts.

Rnd 40: {K2tog, k11, ssk, k5}, rep until 1 st rem, Move marker 1 st to the right. 90 sts.

Rnd 41: {K2tog, k4, S2KP2, k4, ssk, k3}, rep until 1 st rem. Move marker 1 st to the right. 70 sts.

Rnd 42: {K2tog, k9, ssk, k1}, rep. 60 sts.

Rnd 43: {K2tog, yo, k2, S2KP2, k2, yo, ssk, k1}, rep. 50 sts.

Rnd 44: Knit.

Rnd 45: {K2tog, yo, k1, S2KP2, k1, yo, ssk, k1}, rep. 40 sts.

Rnd 46: Move marker 1 st to the left, {K5, S2KP2}, rep. 30 sts.

Rnd 47: {Yo, S2KP2 twice}, rep. 15 sts.

Rnd 48: Knit.

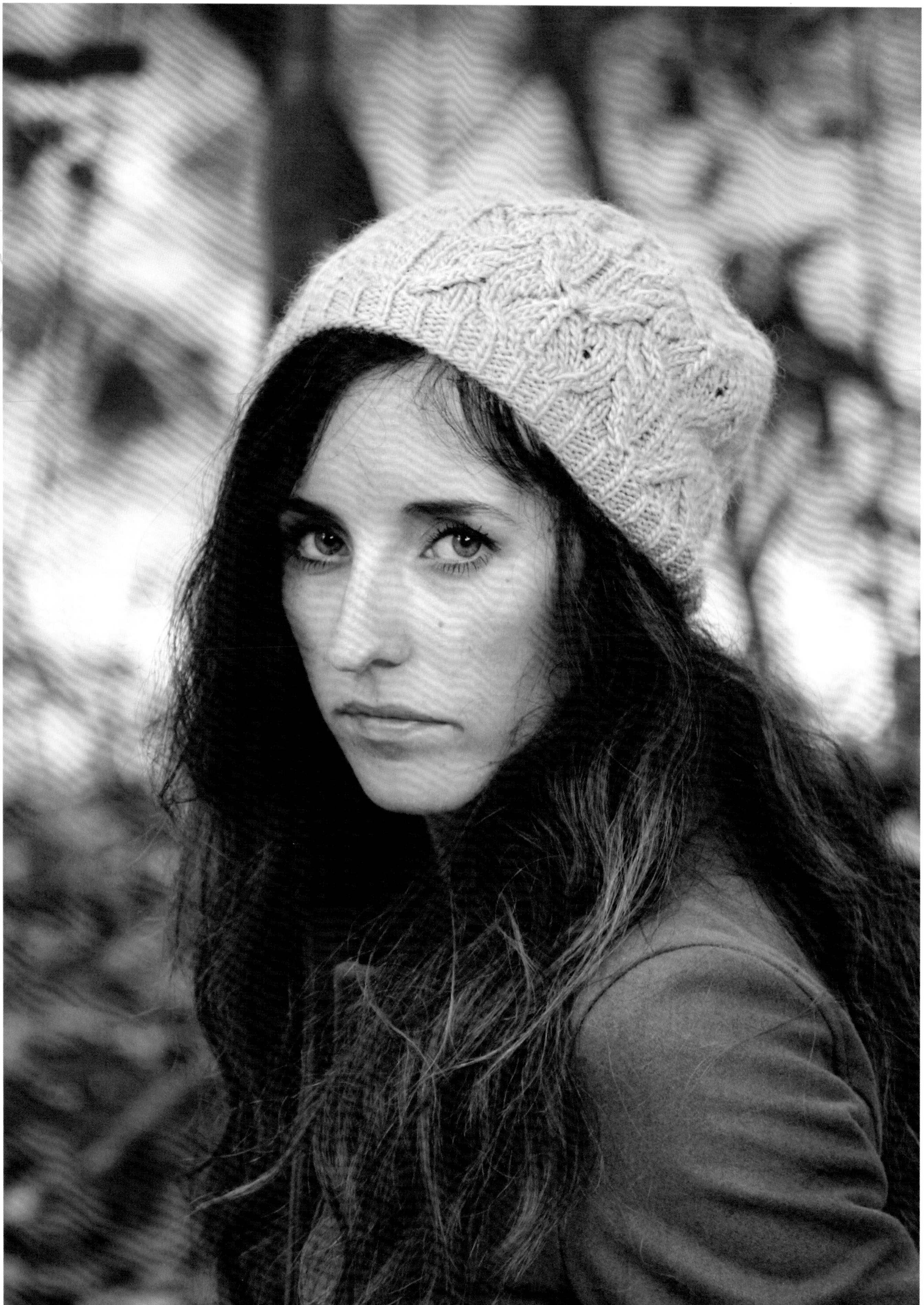

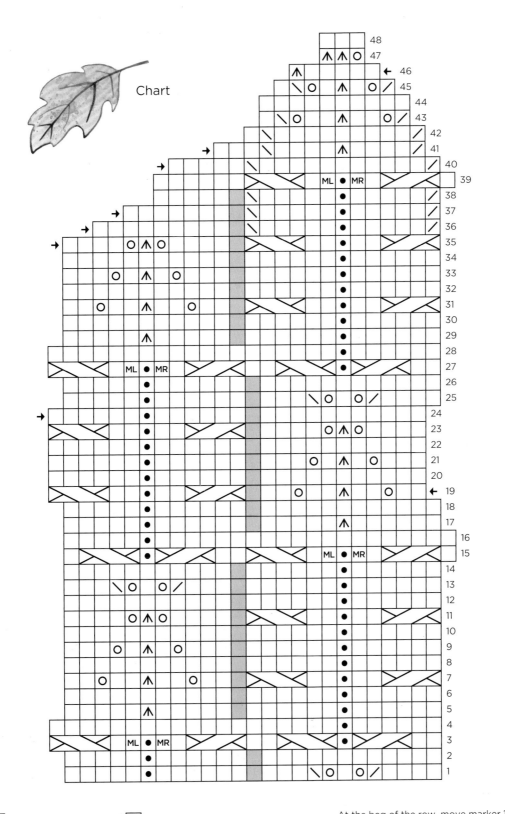

Chart

	knit		yo
•	purl	ML	M1L
/	k2tog	MR	M1R
\	ssk		C4B: Cable 4 Back
Λ	S2KP2		C4F: Cable 4 Front

← At the beg of the row, move marker 1 st to the left: remove marker, sl 1 st from left needle to right needle, replace marker for new beg of rnd.

→ On the LAST patt rep, work until 1 st rem. Move marker 1 st to the right: sl 1 st from left needle to right needle, remove marker, sl 1 st back to left needle, replace marker for new beg of rnd.

no stitch

ivy trellis socks

Lovely ladies' socks adorned with a graceful climbing cable and leaf pattern, like ivy on a trellis. Coordinate your wardrobe with *Ivy Trellis Mittens* on page 72.

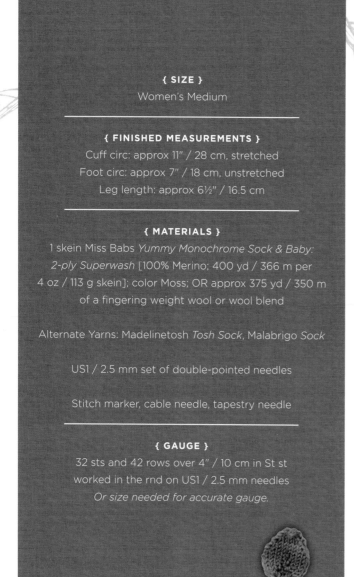

{ SIZE }
Women's Medium

{ FINISHED MEASUREMENTS }
Cuff circ: approx 11" / 28 cm, stretched
Foot circ: approx 7" / 18 cm, unstretched
Leg length: approx 6½" / 16.5 cm

{ MATERIALS }
1 skein Miss Babs *Yummy Monochrome Sock & Baby:
2-ply Superwash* [100% Merino; 400 yd / 366 m per
4 oz / 113 g skein]; color Moss; OR approx 375 yd / 350 m
of a fingering weight wool or wool blend

Alternate Yarns: Madelinetosh *Tosh Sock*, Malabrigo *Sock*

US1 / 2.5 mm set of double-pointed needles

Stitch marker, cable needle, tapestry needle

{ GAUGE }
32 sts and 42 rows over 4" / 10 cm in St st
worked in the rnd on US1 / 2.5 mm needles
Or size needed for accurate gauge.

NOTE: Due to the nature of the stitch pattern, the leg of this sock does not have much stretch. If you are needing extra room, consider going up a needle size on the leg portion.

Cuff

CO 66 sts onto 1 dpn. Divide the sts evenly among 3 dpns: 22 sts on each needle. Pm and join in the rnd, being careful not to twist sts.

Ribbing setup rnd: {K1-tbl, p1}, rep.

Work even in est rib patt for 1½" / 4 cm from CO edge.

Leg

Setup rnd: {K2, p2, k1, p2, k2, p4, k5, p4}, rep.

Begin Chart A and work rnds 1–16 3 times total, then work rnds 1–8 once more.

HEEL FLAP

P1, work back and forth across next 33 sts as follows:

Row 1 (RS): Sl 1, {p1, k1-tbl}, rep.
Row 2 (WS): Sl 1, {k1, p1}, rep.

Cont in est rib patt for 27 rows more. End on a RS row.

TURN HEEL

Row 1 (WS): Sl 1, p17, p2tog, p1, turn.
Row 2 (RS): Sl 1, k4, ssk, k1, turn.
Row 3: Sl 1, p5, p2tog, p1, turn.
Row 4: Sl 1, k6, ssk, k1, turn.
Row 5: Sl 1, p7, p2tog, p1, turn.
Row 6: Sl 1, k8, ssk, k1, turn.
Row 7: Sl 1, p9, p2tog, p1, turn.
Row 8: Sl 1, k10, ssk, k1, turn.
Row 9: Sl 1, p11, p2tog, p1, turn.
Row 10: Sl 1, k12, ssk, k1, turn.
Row 11: Sl 1, p13, p2tog, p1, turn.
Row 12: Sl 1, k14, ssk, k1, turn.
Row 13: Sl 1, p15, p2tog, p1, turn. 20 sts.

GUSSET

Sl 1, k9. With new dpn (needle 1), k7, ssk, k1, pick up and knit 15 sts along the right side of the heel flap in the back loop of the sl sts. 15 picked up sts, 24 sts total on needle 1.

With next dpn (needle 2), M1 in corner between gusset and instep sts, k3, p2, k1, p2, k2, p4, ssk, k1, k2tog, p4, k2, p2, k1, p2, k3, M1 in corner between gusset and instep sts. 33 sts on needle 2.

With next dpn (needle 3), pick up and knit 15 sts along left side of heel flap in the back loop of the sl sts, k10 heel sts. 15 picked up sts, 25 sts total on needle 3. Pm. The beg of the rnd is now at the center of the heel.

82 sts: 24 sts on needle 1, 33 sts on needle 2, 25 sts on needle 3.

Next rnd: *Needle 1:* K9, k15 tbl; *Needle 2:* Work rnd 2 of Chart B; *Needle 3:* K15 tbl, k10.

Dec rnd: *Needle 1:* Knit until 2 sts rem, k2tog; *Needle 2:* Work even across instep sts in est patt; *Needle 3:* Ssk, knit to end. 2 sts dec.

Cont working instep sts in est patt and work sole sts in St st, rep dec rnd every other rnd until 31 sole sts rem: 15 sts on needle 1, 33 sts on needle 2, 16 sts on needle 3.

Foot

Work even as est, working sole sts in St st and instep sts in est patt, until foot of sock measures 2" / 5 cm less than total foot length ending on either Rnd 8 or Rnd 16.

NOTE: If ending on Rnd 8, work final Rnd 8 over sts on needle 2 as follows: K4, p2tog, p2, ssk, k1, k2tog, p2, p2tog, k2, p2, Dec-5, p2, k2, p2tog, p2, ssk, k1, k2tog, p2, p2tog, k4. 35 sts.

Redistribute sts as follows. Sl 1 instep st from each end of needle 2 to the sole portion of the sock on needles 1 and 3. 66 sts: 33 instep sts, 33 sole sts: 16 sts on needle 1, 33 sts on needle 2, 17 sts on needle 3.

Toe

Next rnd: *Needle 1:* Knit across; *Needle 2:* K2tog, knit to end; *Needle 3:* K2tog, knit to end.

64 sts: 32 sts on needle 2 and 16 sts each on needles 1 and 3.

Dec rnd: *Needle 1:* Knit until 3 sts rem, k2tog, k1; *Needle 2:* K1, ssk, knit until 3 sts rem, k2tog, k1; *Needle 3:* K1, ssk, knit to end. 4 sts dec.

Rep dec rnd every other rnd until 32 sts total rem: 16 sts on needle 2 and 8 sts each on needles 1 and 3.

Rep dec rnd every rnd until 12 sts total rem: 6 sts on needle 2 and 3 sts each on needles 1 and 3.

Knit sts on needle 1 only. Remove marker. Cut yarn leaving a long tail. Graft rem toe sts together using the kitchener st.

Finishing

Weave in all ends on the WS. Wet block to measurements.

Chart A (WORKED 3 TIMES AROUND)

Rnd 1: K2, p2, k1, p2, k2, p4, ssk, k1, k2tog, p4. 20 sts.

Rnd 2: K2, p2, Inc-3, p2, k2, p4, k3, p4, rep. 22 sts.

Rnd 3: K2, pfb, p1, k1, yo, p1, yo, k1, p1, pfb, k2, p4, S2KP2, p4, rep. 24 sts.

Sl 2 sts to the right as follows: Sl 2 sts from left needle to right needle; rep for 2nd and 3rd dpns. 24 sts on each needle.

Rnd 4: P3, k2, p1, k2, p3, C4F, P5, C4B.

Rnd 5: Pfb, p2, k2, yo, p1, yo, k2, p2, pfb, k4, p5, k4. 28 sts.

Rnd 6: P4, k3, p1, k3, p4, k2, T4F, p1, T4B, k2.

Rnd 7: P4, ssk, k3, k2tog, p4, k2, p2, k2, p1, k2, p2, k2. 26 sts.

Rnd 8: P4, k5, p4, k2, p2, Dec-5, p2, k2. 22 sts.

Rnd 9: P4, ssk, k1, k2tog, p4, k2, p2, k1, p2, k2. 20 sts.

Rnd 10: P4, k3, p4, k2, p2, Inc-3, p2, k2. 22 sts.

Rnd 11: P4, S2KP2, p4, k2, pfb, p1, k1, yo, p1, yo, k1, p1, pfb, k2. On last rep, do not work last k2. 24 sts.

Slip 2 sts to the left as follows: Sl last 2 sts to next needle; rep for 2nd and 3rd dpns. 24 sts on each needle.

Rnd 12: C4F, p5, C4B, p3, k2, p1, k2, p3.

Rnd 13: K4, p5, k4, pfb, p2, k2, yo, p1, yo, k2, p2, pfb. 28 sts.

Rnd 14: K2, T4F, p1, T4B, k2, p4, k3, p1, k3, p4.

Rnd 15: K2, p2, k2, p1, k2, p2, k2, p4, ssk, k3, k2tog, p4. 26 sts.

Rnd 16: K2, p2, Dec-5, p2, k2, p4, k5, p4. 22 sts.

Chart B

Rnd 1: K4, p2, k1, p2, k2, p4, ssk, k1, k2tog, p4, k2, p2, k1, p2, k4. 33 sts.

Rnd 2: K4, p2, Inc-3, p2, k2, p4, k3, p4, k2, p2, Inc-3, p2, k4. 37 sts.

Rnd 3: K4, pfb, p1, k1, yo, p1, yo, k1, p1, pfb, k2, p4, S2KP2, p4, k2, pfb, p1, k1, yo, p1, yo, k1, p1, pfb, k4. 43 sts.

Rnd 4: C4B, p3, k2, p1, k2, p3, C4F, p5, C4B, p3, k2, p1, k2, p3, C4F.

Rnd 5: K4, pfb, p2, k2, yo, p1, yo, k2, p2, pfb, k4, p5, k4, pfb, p2, k2, yo, p1, yo, k2, p2, pfb, k4. 51 sts.

Rnd 6: K4, p4, k3, p1, k3, p4, k2, T4F, p1, T4B, k2, p4, k3, p1, k3, p4, k4.

Rnd 7: K4, p4, ssk, k3, k2tog, p4, k2, p2, k2, p1, k2, p2, k2, p4, ssk, k3, k2tog, p4, k4. 47 sts.

Rnd 8: K4, p4, k5, p4, k2, p2, Dec-5, p2, k2, p4, k5, p4, k4. 43 sts.

Rnd 9: K4, p4, ssk, k1, k2tog, p4, k2, p2, k1, p2, k2, p4, ssk, k1, k2tog, p4, k4. 39 sts.

Rnd 10: K4, p4, k3, p4, k2, p2, Inc-3, p2, k2, p4, k3, p4, k4. 41 sts.

Rnd 11: K4, p4, S2KP2, p4, k2, pfb, p1, k1, yo, p1, yo, k1, p1, pfb, k2, p4, S2KP2, p4, k4.

Rnd 12: K2, C4F, p5, C4B, p3, k2, p1, k2, p3, C4F, p5, C4B, k2.

Rnd 13: K6, p5, k4, pfb, p2, k2, yo, p1, yo, k2, p2, pfb, k4, p5, k6. 45 sts.

Rnd 14: K4, T4F, p1, T4B, k2, p4, k3, p1, k3, p4, k2, T4F, p1, T4B, k4.

Rnd 15: K4, p2, k2, p1, k2, p2, k2, p4, ssk, k3, k2tog, p4, k2, p2, k2, p1, k2, p2, k4. 43 sts.

Rnd 16: K4, p2, Dec-5, p2, k2, p4, k5, p4, k2, p2, Dec-5, p2, k4. 35 sts.

Chart A

Chart B

☐ knit	⧅	C4B: Cable 4 Back
⊡ purl	⧄	C4F: Cable 4 Front
⊙ yo	⧅	T4B: Twist 4 Back
⟋ k2tog	⧄	T4F: Twist 4 Front
⟍ ssk	←	Sl 2 sts to the left as follows: Sl last 2 sts to next needle.
⋀ S2KP2		
⋀₅ Dec-5	→	Sl 2 sts to the right as follows: Before working round, sl 2 sts from left needle to right needle; rep for each dpn.
ⱱ pfb		
ⱱ₃ Inc-3	▨	no stitch

twin leaf loop

A long, lacy loop of leaves that looks great
doubled around your neck and worn as a cowl.

{ FINISHED MEASUREMENTS }
Width: 6" / 15 cm
Length: 42" / 106.5 cm

{ MATERIALS }
2 skeins The Fibre Company *Tundra* [60% Baby Alpaca,
30% Merino Wool, 10% Silk; 120 yd / 110 m per 3½ oz /
100 g skein] in Mink OR approx 175 yd / 150 m
of a bulky weight wool or wool blend

Alternate Yarn: Misti Alpaca *Chunky*

US11 / 8 mm straight needles

Tapestry needle

{ GAUGE }
12 sts and 16 rows over 4" / 10 cm in St st
on US11 / 8 mm needles
Or size needed for accurate gauge.

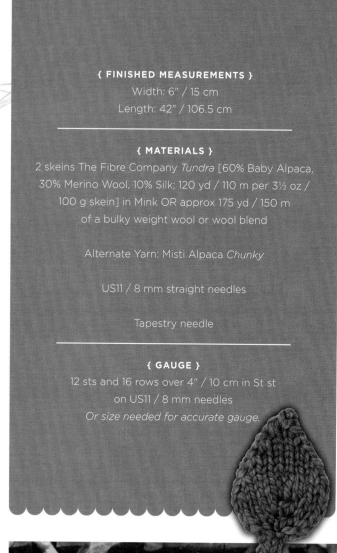

Pattern

CO 23 sts.

Purl 1 WS row.

Begin chart patt and work rnds 1–12, 14 times total.

Piece measures approx 42" / 106.5 cm.

BO all sts.

Finishing

Cut yarn. Wet block.

Seam BO edge to CO edge using yarn tails and tapestry needle.

Weave in all ends on the WS.

Chart

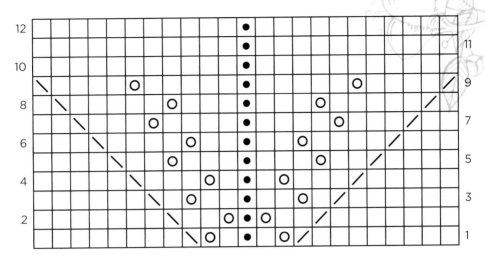

- ☐ knit RS rows, purl WS rows
- ● purl RS rows, knit WS rows
- ⊙ yo
- ╱ k2tog RS rows, p2tog WS rows
- ╲ ssk RS rows, p2tog-tbl WS rows

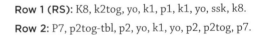

Row 1 (RS): K8, k2tog, yo, k1, p1, k1, yo, ssk, k8.
Row 2: P7, p2tog-tbl, p2, yo, k1, yo, p2, p2tog, p7.
Row 3: K6, k2tog, k1, yo, k2, p1, k2, yo, k1, ssk, k6.
Row 4: P5, p2tog-tbl, p3, yo, p1, k1, p1, yo, p3, p2tog, p5.
Row 5: K4, k2tog, k2, yo, k3, p1, k3, yo, k2, ssk, k4.
Row 6: P3, p2tog-tbl, p4, yo, p2, k1, p2, yo, p4, p2tog, p3.
Row 7: K2, k2tog, k3, yo, k4, p1, k4, yo, k3, ssk, k2.
Row 8: P1, p2tog-tbl, p5, yo, p3, k1, p3, yo, p5, p2tog, p1.
Row 9: K2tog, k4, yo, k5, p1, k5, yo, k4, ssk.
Row 10: P11, k1, p11.
Row 11: K11, p1, k11.
Row 12: As for Row 10.

ivy trellis mittens.

Beautiful textured mittens to match the *Ivy Trellis Socks* on page 62.

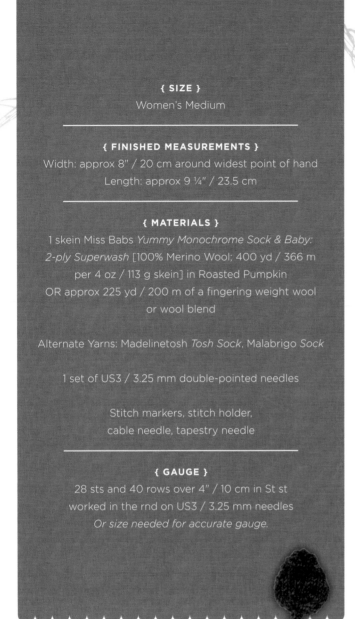

{ SIZE }
Women's Medium

—

{ FINISHED MEASUREMENTS }
Width: approx 8" / 20 cm around widest point of hand
Length: approx 9 ¼" / 23.5 cm

—

{ MATERIALS }
1 skein Miss Babs *Yummy Monochrome Sock & Baby:
2-ply Superwash* [100% Merino Wool; 400 yd / 366 m
per 4 oz / 113 g skein] in Roasted Pumpkin
OR approx 225 yd / 200 m of a fingering weight wool
or wool blend

Alternate Yarns: Madelinetosh *Tosh Sock*, Malabrigo *Sock*

1 set of US3 / 3.25 mm double-pointed needles

Stitch markers, stitch holder,
cable needle, tapestry needle

—

{ GAUGE }
28 sts and 40 rows over 4" / 10 cm in St st
worked in the rnd on US3 / 3.25 mm needles
Or size needed for accurate gauge.

Cuff

CO 54 sts onto 1 dpn. Divide the sts evenly between 3 dpns. Pm and join in the rnd, being careful not to twist your sts.

Ribbing setup rnd: {K1-tbl, p1}, rep.

Work even in est rib patt until piece measures 2" / 5 cm from CO edge.

Hand

Setup rnd: K2, pm, k2, p2, k1, p2, k2, p4, k5, p4, k2, p2, k1, p2, k2, pm, k8, M1R, k7, M1L, k6. 56 sts.
Rnd 1: K2, work row 1 of Chart A over 31 sts, knit to end of rnd.
Rnds 2-18: Work rows 2–16 of Chart A, then work rows 1–2 once more.

LEFT MITTEN ONLY

Rnd 19: K1, M1R, k1, M1L, work row 3 of Chart A, knit to end of rnd.
Rnd 20: Knit to marker, work row 4 of Chart A working k2 instead of C4B* at beg of chart sts, knit to end of rnd.
Rnd 21: K1, M1R, k3, M1L, work row 5 of Chart A, knit to end of rnd.
Rnd 22 and all even rnds: Knit to marker, work next row of chart, knit to end of rnd.

Rnd 23: K1, M1R, k5, M1L, work row 7 of Chart A, knit to end of rnd.
Rnd 25: K1, M1R, k7, M1L, work row 9 of Chart A, knit to end of rnd.
Rnd 27: K1, M1R, k9, M1L, work row 11 of Chart A, knit to end of rnd.
Rnd 29: K1, M1R, k11, M1L, work row 13 of Chart A, knit to end of rnd.
Rnd 31: K1, M1R, k13, M1L, work row 15 of Chart A, knit to end of rnd.
Rnd 33: K1, M1R, k15, M1L, work row 1 of Chart A, knit to end of rnd.
Rnd 35: K1, M1R, k17, M1L, work row 3 of Chart A, knit to end of rnd.
Rnd 36: Knit to 2 sts before marker, work row 4 of Chart A, knit to end of rnd.
Rnd 37: K1, slide next 19 gusset sts to holder to be worked later. Using backwards loop cast-on method, CO 1 st, work row 5 of Chart A, knit to end of rnd.

RIGHT MITTEN ONLY

Rnd 19: K2, work row 3 of Chart A, M1R, k1, M1L, knit to end of rnd.
Rnd 20: Work row 4 of Chart A, working k2 instead of C4F* at end of chart sts, knit to end of rnd.
Rnd 21: K2, work row 5 of Chart A, M1R, k3, M1L, knit to end of rnd.
Rnd 22 and all even rnds: K2, work next row of Chart A, knit to end of rnd.
Rnd 23: K2, work row 7 of Chart A, M1R, k5, M1L, knit to end of rnd.
Rnd 25: K2, work row 9 of Chart A, M1R, k7, M1L, knit to end of rnd.
Rnd 27: K2, work row 11 of Chart A, M1R, k9, M1L, knit to end of rnd.
Rnd 29: K2, work row 13 of Chart A, M1R, k11, M1L, knit to end of rnd.
Rnd 31: K2, work row 15 of Chart A, M1R, k13, M1L, knit to end of rnd.
Rnd 33: K2, work row 1 of Chart A, M1R, k15, M1L, knit to end of rnd.
Rnd 35: K2, work row 3 of Chart A, M1R, k17, M1L, knit to end of rnd.
Rnd 36: Work row 4 of Chart A, knit to end of rnd.
Rnd 37: K2, work row 5 of Chart A, slide next 19 gusset sts to holder to be worked later. Using backwards loop cast on method, CO 1 st, knit to end of rnd.

BOTH MITTENS

Rnd 38: K2, work row 6 of Chart A, knit to end of rnd.
Rnds 39-63: Work rows 7–16 of Chart A, then work rows 1–15 once more.
Rnd 64: K2, work row 1 of Chart B, knit to end of rnd.
Rnd 65: Move marker 2 sts to the left by removing marker, sl 2 sts from left needle to right needle, replace marker for new beg of rnd.

Work row 2 of Chart B over 31 sts, pm, ssk, knit to last 2 sts, k2tog.

Rnd 66: Work next row of Chart B to marker, knit to end of rnd.
Rnd 67: Work next row of Chart B to marker, ssk, knit to last 2 sts, k2tog. 2 sts dec outside of chart sts.
Rnd 68: As for rnd 66.
Rnds 69–75: As for rnd 67.
Rnd 76: As for rnd 66. 14 sts total.

Divide rem sts evenly between 2 dpns. Cut yarn leaving a long tail. Graft sts together using the kitchener st.

Thumb

Divide 19 held thumb sts evenly among 3 dpns.

Next rnd: K19, pick up and knit 3 sts where thumb meets hand, sl 1, pm to mark the beg of rnd. 22 sts.

Next rnd: K17, ssk, k1, k2tog. 20 sts.

Work even until thumb measures 1½" / 4 cm from joining row or approx ½" / 1.5 cm less than desired final length.

Next rnd: {K3, k2tog}, rep. 16 sts.
Next rnd: {K2, k2tog}, rep. 12 sts.
Next rnd: {K1, k2tog}, rep. 8 sts.
Next rnd: K2tog, rep. 4 sts.

Remove marker. Cut yarn, thread tail onto tapestry needle, pass through rem 4 live sts and cinch to close.

Finishing

Weave in ends on the WS. Wet block.

Chart A

16
15
14
13
12
11
10
9
8
7
6
5
4
3
2
1

Chart B

13
12
11
10
9
8
7
6
5
4
3
2
1

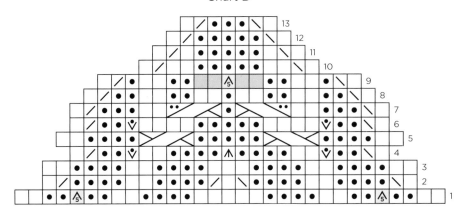

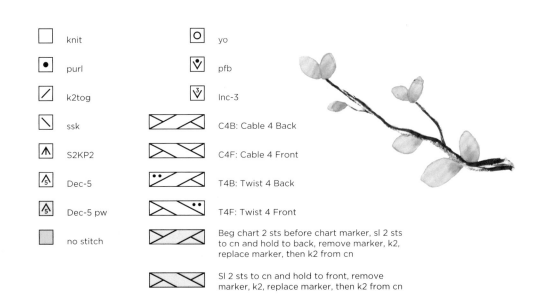

	knit		yo
•	purl	⋁	pfb
/	k2tog	⋁₃	Inc-3
\	ssk		C4B: Cable 4 Back
⋀	S2KP2		C4F: Cable 4 Front
⋀₅	Dec-5	••	T4B: Twist 4 Back
⋀₅	Dec-5 pw	••	T4F: Twist 4 Front
	no stitch		Beg chart 2 sts before chart marker, sl 2 sts to cn and hold to back, remove marker, k2, replace marker, then k2 from cn
			Sl 2 sts to cn and hold to front, remove marker, k2, replace marker, then k2 from cn

Chart A

Rnd 1: K2, p2, k1, p2, k2, p4, ssk, k1, k2tog, p4, k2, p2, k1, p2, k2. 29 sts.

Rnd 2: K2, p2, Inc-3, p2, k2, p4, k3, p4, k2, p2, Inc-3, p2, k2. 33 sts.

Rnd 3: K2, pfb, p1, k1, yo, p1, yo, k1, p1, pfb, k2, p4, S2KP2, p4, k2, pfb, p1, k1, yo, p1, yo, k1, p1, pfb, k2. 39 sts.

NOTE: Rnd 4 begins 2 sts before the marker for the beg of chart and ends 2 sts after the marker for the end of chart. Replace markers as follows: for C4B* – sl 2 sts to cn and hold to back, remove marker, k2, replace marker, then k2 from cn; for C4F* – sl 2 sts to cn and hold to front, remove marker, k2, replace marker, then k2 from cn.

Rnd 4: C4B*, p3, k2, p1, k2, p3, C4F, p5, C4B, p3, k2, p1, k2, p3, C4F*.

Rnd 5: K2, pfb, p2, k2, yo, p1, yo, k2, p2, pfb, k4, p5, k4, pfb, p2, k2, yo, p1, yo, k2, p2, pfb, k2. 47 sts.

Rnd 6: K2, p4, k3, p1, k3, p4, k2, T4F, p1, T4B, k2, p4, k3, p1, k3, p4, k2.

Rnd 7: K2, p4, ssk, k3, k2tog, p4, k2, p2, k2, p1, k2, p2, k2, p4, ssk, k3, k2tog, p4, k2. 43 sts.

Rnd 8: K2, p4, k5, p4, k2, p2, Dec-5, p2, k2, p4, k5, p4, k2. 39 sts.

Rnd 9: K2, p4, ssk, k1, k2tog, p4, k2, p2, k1, p2, k2, p4, ssk, k1, k2tog, p4, k2. 35 sts.

Rnd 10: K2, p4, k3, p4, k2, p2, Inc-3, p2, k2, p4, k3, p4, k2. 37 sts.

Rnd 11: K2, p4, S2KP2, p4, k2, pfb, p1, k1, yo, p1, yo, k1, p1, pfb, k2, p4, S2KP2, p4, k2.

Rnd 12: C4F, p5, C4B, p3, k2, p1, k2, p3, C4F, p5, C4B.

Rnd 13: K4, p5, k4, pfb, p2, k2, yo, p1, yo, k2, p2, pfb, k4, p5, k4. 41 sts.

Rnd 14: K2, T4F, p1, T4B, k2, p4, k3, p1, k3, p4, k2, T4F, p1, T4B, k2.

Rnd 15: K2, p2, k2, p1, k2, p2, k2, p4, ssk, k3, k2tog, p4, k2, p2, k2, p1, k2, p2, k2. 39 sts.

Rnd 16: K2, p2, Dec-5, p2, k2, p4, k5, p4, k2, p2, Dec-5, p2, k2. 31 sts.

Rep rnds 1–16 for patt.

Chart B

Rnd 1: K2, p2, Dec-5 pw, p2, k2, p4, k5, p4, k2, p2, Dec-5 pw, p2, k2. 31 sts.

Rnd 2: K1, ssk, p4, k2, p4, ssk, k1, k2tog, p4, k2, p4, k2tog, k1. 27 sts.

Rnd 3: K2, p4, k2, p4, k3, p4, k2, p4, k2.

Rnd 4: K1, ssk, p2, pfb, k2, p4, S2KP2, p4, k2, pfb, p2, k2tog, k1. 25 sts.

Rnd 5: K2, p4, C4F, p5, C4B, p4, k2.

Rnd 6: K1, ssk, p2, pfb, k4, p5, k4, pfb, p2, k2tog, k1.

Rnd 7: K1, ssk, p3, k2, T4F, p1, T4B, k2, p3, k2tog, k1. 23 sts.

Rnd 8: K1, ssk, {p2, k2} twice, p1, {k2, p2} twice, k2tog, k1. 21 sts.

Rnd 9: K1, ssk, p1, k2, p2, Dec-5 pw, p2, k2, p1, k2tog, k1. 15 sts.

Rnd 10: K1, ssk, k2, p5, k2, k2tog, k1. 13 sts.

Rnd 11: K1, ssk, k1, p5, k1, k2tog, k1. 11 sts.

Rnd 12: K1, ssk, p5, k2tog, k1. 9 sts.

Rnd 13: K1, ssk, p3, k2tog, k1. 7 sts.

pressed leaves

This romantic beret features a lovely stitch pattern
reminiscent of leaves pressed between the pages of a book.

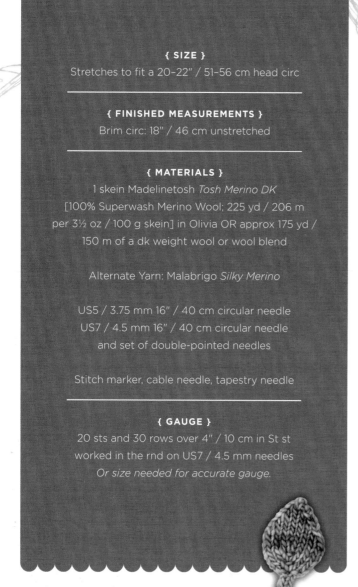

{ SIZE }
Stretches to fit a 20–22" / 51–56 cm head circ

{ FINISHED MEASUREMENTS }
Brim circ: 18" / 46 cm unstretched

{ MATERIALS }
1 skein Madelinetosh *Tosh Merino DK*
[100% Superwash Merino Wool; 225 yd / 206 m
per 3½ oz / 100 g skein] in Olivia OR approx 175 yd /
150 m of a dk weight wool or wool blend

Alternate Yarn: Malabrigo *Silky Merino*

US5 / 3.75 mm 16" / 40 cm circular needle
US7 / 4.5 mm 16" / 40 cm circular needle
and set of double-pointed needles

Stitch marker, cable needle, tapestry needle

{ GAUGE }
20 sts and 30 rows over 4" / 10 cm in St st
worked in the rnd on US7 / 4.5 mm needles
Or size needed for accurate gauge.

Brim

CO 120 sts onto smaller circular needle. Pm, join for working in the rnd being careful not to twist your sts.

Ribbing setup rnd: {K1-tbl, p1}, rep to end.

Work in est rib patt for 1½" / 4 cm.

Switch to larger circular needle.

Work rnds 1–49 of chart patt. Switch to dpns when work becomes too tight on the circular needle.

Next rnd: {K2tog tbl}, rep. 6 sts.

Rep last rnd once more. 3 sts.

Remove marker. Work 2 rnds of I-cord.

Finishing

Cut yarn, thread tail onto tapestry needle, pass through rem 3 live sts and cinch to close. Weave in all ends on the WS. Wet block, stretching over a dinner plate to dry.

Chart (WORKED 6 TIMES AROUND)

Rnd 1: {K1-tbl, pfb, p4, k1-tbl, p4, pfb, (k1-tbl, p3) twice}, rep. 132 sts.

Rnd 2: {T2F-tbl, p5, k1-tbl, p5, T2B-tbl, p3, k1-tbl, p3}, rep.

Rnd 3: {P1, T2F-tbl, p9, T2B-tbl, p4, k1-tbl, p3}, rep.

Rnd 4: {P2, T2F-tbl, p7, T2B-tbl, p5, Inc-3, p3}, rep. 144 sts.

Rnd 5: {P3, T2F-tbl, p5, T2B-tbl, p4, T3BR-tbl, k1-tbl, T3FL-tbl, p1}, rep.

Rnd 6: Move marker 1 st to the left: remove marker, sl 1 st from left needle to right needle, replace marker for new beg of rnd. {P3, T2F-tbl, p3, T2B-tbl, p3, T3BR-tbl, p2, k1-tbl, p2, T3FL-tbl}, rep.

Rnd 7: Move marker 1 st to the left, {p3, T2F-tbl, p1, T2B-tbl, p3, T2B-tbl, p2, p2tog, Inc-3, p2tog, p2, T2F-tbl}, rep.

Rnd 8: {P4, sssk, p4, k1-tbl, p2, T3BR-tbl, k1-tbl, T3FL-tbl, p2, k1-tbl}, rep. 132 sts.

Rnd 9: Move marker 1 st to the left, {p7, T2B-tbl, p1, T2B-tbl, p2, k1-tbl, p2, T2F-tbl, p1, T2F-tbl}, rep.

Rnd 10: {P7, k1-tbl, p4, p2tog, Inc-3, p2tog, p4, k1-tbl}, rep.

Rnd 11: {P7, k1-tbl, p4, T2B-tbl, k1-tbl, T2F-tbl, p4, k1-tbl}, rep.

Rnd 12: {(P3, k1-tbl) twice, (p6, k1-tbl) twice}, rep.

Rnd 13: {P3, k1-tbl, p3, T2F-tbl, p5, k1-tbl, p5, T2B-tbl}, rep.

Rnd 14: {P3, k1-tbl, p4, T2F-tbl, p9, T2B-tbl, p1}, rep.

Rnd 15: {P3, Inc-3, p5, T2F-tbl, p7, T2B-tbl, p2}, rep. 144 sts.

Rnd 16: {P1, T3BR-tbl, k1-tbl, T3FL-tbl, p4, T2F-tbl, p5, T2B-tbl, p3}, rep until 1 st remains. Move marker 1 st to the right: sl 1 st from left needle to right needle, remove marker, sl 1 st back to left needle, replace marker for new beg of rnd.

Rnd 17: {T3BR-tbl, p2, k1-tbl, p2, T3FL-tbl, p3, T2F-tbl, p3, T2B-tbl, p3}, rep until 1 st remains, move marker 1 st to the right.

Rnd 18: {T2B-tbl, p2, p2tog, Inc-3, p2tog, p2, T2F-tbl, p3, T2F-tbl, p1, T2B-tbl, p3}, rep.

Rnd 19: {K1-tbl, p2, T3BR-tbl, k1-tbl, T3FL-tbl, p2, k1-tbl, p4, sssk, p4}, rep until 1 st remains, move marker 1 st to the right. 132 sts.

Rnd 20: {T2B-tbl, p1, T2B-tbl, p2, k1-tbl, p2, T2F-tbl, p1, T2F-tbl, p7}, rep.

Rnd 21: {K1-tbl, p4, p2tog, Inc-3, p2tog, p4, k1-tbl, p7}, rep.

Rnd 22: {K1-tbl, p4, T2B-tbl, k1-tbl, T2F-tbl, p4, k1-tbl, p7}, rep.

Rnd 23: {(K1-tbl, p6) twice, (k1-tbl, p3) twice}, rep.

Rnd 24: {T2F-tbl, p5, k1-tbl, p5, T2B-tbl, p3, k1-tbl, p3}, rep.

Rnd 25: {P1, T2F-tbl, p9, T2B-tbl, p4, k1-tbl, p3}, rep.

Rnd 26: {P2, T2F-tbl, p7, T2B-tbl, p5, Inc-3, p3}, rep. 144 sts.

Rnd 27: {P3, T2F-tbl, p5, T2B-tbl, p4, T3BR-tbl, k1-tbl, T3FL-tbl, p1}, rep.

Rnd 28: Move marker 1 st to the left, {p3, T2F-tbl, p3, T2B-tbl, p3, T3BR-tbl, p2, k1-tbl, p2, T3FL-tbl}, rep.

Rnd 29: Move marker 1 st to the left, {p3, T2F-tbl, p1, T2B-tbl, p3, T2B-tbl, p2, p2tog, Inc-3, p2tog, p2, T2F-tbl}, rep.

Rnd 30: {P4, sssk, p4, k1-tbl, p2, T3BR-tbl, k1-tbl, T3FL-tbl, p2, k1-tbl}, rep. 132 sts.

Rnd 31: Move marker 1 st to the left, {p7, T2B-tbl, p1, T2B-tbl, p2, k1-tbl, p2, T2F-tbl, p1, T2F-tbl}, rep.

Rnd 32: {P7, k1-tbl, p4, p2tog, Inc-3, p2tog, p4, k1-tbl}, rep.

Rnd 33: {P7, k1-tbl, p4, T2B-tbl, k1-tbl, T2F-tbl, p4, k1-tbl}, rep.

Rnd 34: {(P3, k1-tbl) twice, (p6, k1-tbl) twice}, rep.

Rnd 35: {P3, k1-tbl, p3, T2F-tbl, p5, k1-tbl, p5, T2B-tbl}, rep.

Rnd 36: {P3, k1-tbl, p4, T2F-tbl, p9, T2B-tbl, p1}, rep.

Rnd 37: {P1, p2tog, k1-tbl, p2tog, p3, T2F-tbl, p7, T2B-tbl, p2}, rep. 120 sts.

Rnd 38: {P2, k1-tbl, p5, T2F-tbl, p5, T2B-tbl, p3}, rep.

Rnd 39: {P2tog, k1-tbl, p2tog, p4, T2F-tbl, p3, T2B-tbl, p4}, rep. 108 sts.

Rnd 40: {P1, k1-tbl, p6, T2F-tbl, p1, T2B-tbl, p5}, rep.

Rnd 41: Move marker 1 st to the left, {k1-tbl, p2tog, p5, sssk, p5, p2tog}, rep. 84 sts.

Rnd 42: {K1-tbl, p13}, rep.

Rnd 43: {K1-tbl, p2tog, p9, p2tog}, rep. 72 sts.

Rnd 44: {K1-tbl, p2tog, p7, p2tog}, rep. 60 sts.

Rnd 45: {K1-tbl, p2tog, p5, p2tog}, rep. 48 sts.

Rnd 46: {K1-tbl, p2tog, p3, p2tog}, rep. 36 sts.

Rnd 47: {K1-tbl, p2tog, p1, p2tog}, rep. 24 sts.

Rnd 48: {K1-tbl, p2tog, p1}, rep. 18 sts.

Rnd 49: {K1-tbl, p2tog}, rep. 12 sts.

☐	knit	
⊡	purl	
⏣	k1-tbl	
⬕	p2tog	
◩	sssk	
ⱴ	pfb	
ⱴ³	Inc-3	
▨	no stitch	

T2B-tbl: Twist 2 Back through the back loop. Sl 1 st to cn and hold to back. K1-tbl from left needle, then p1 from cn.

T2F-tbl: Twist 2 Front through the back loop. Sl 1 st to cn and hold to front. P1 from left needle, then k1-tbl from cn.

T3BR-tbl: Twist 3 Back Right through the back loop. Sl 2 sts to cn and hold to back. K1-tbl from left needle, then p2 from cn.

T3FL-tbl: Twist 3 Front Left through the back loop. Sl 1 st to cn and hold to front. P2 from left needle, then k1-tbl from cn.

← At the beg of the row, move marker 1 st to the left: remove marker, sl 1 st from left needle to right needle, replace marker for new beg of rnd.

→ On the LAST patt rep, work until 1 st rem. Move marker 1 st to the right: sl 1 st from left needle to right needle, remove marker, sl 1 st back to left needle, replace marker for new beg of rnd.

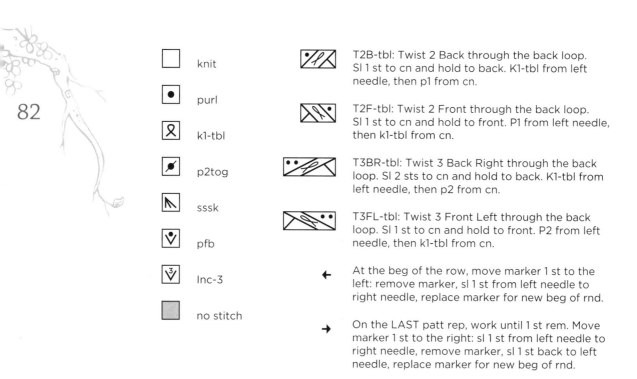

Chart

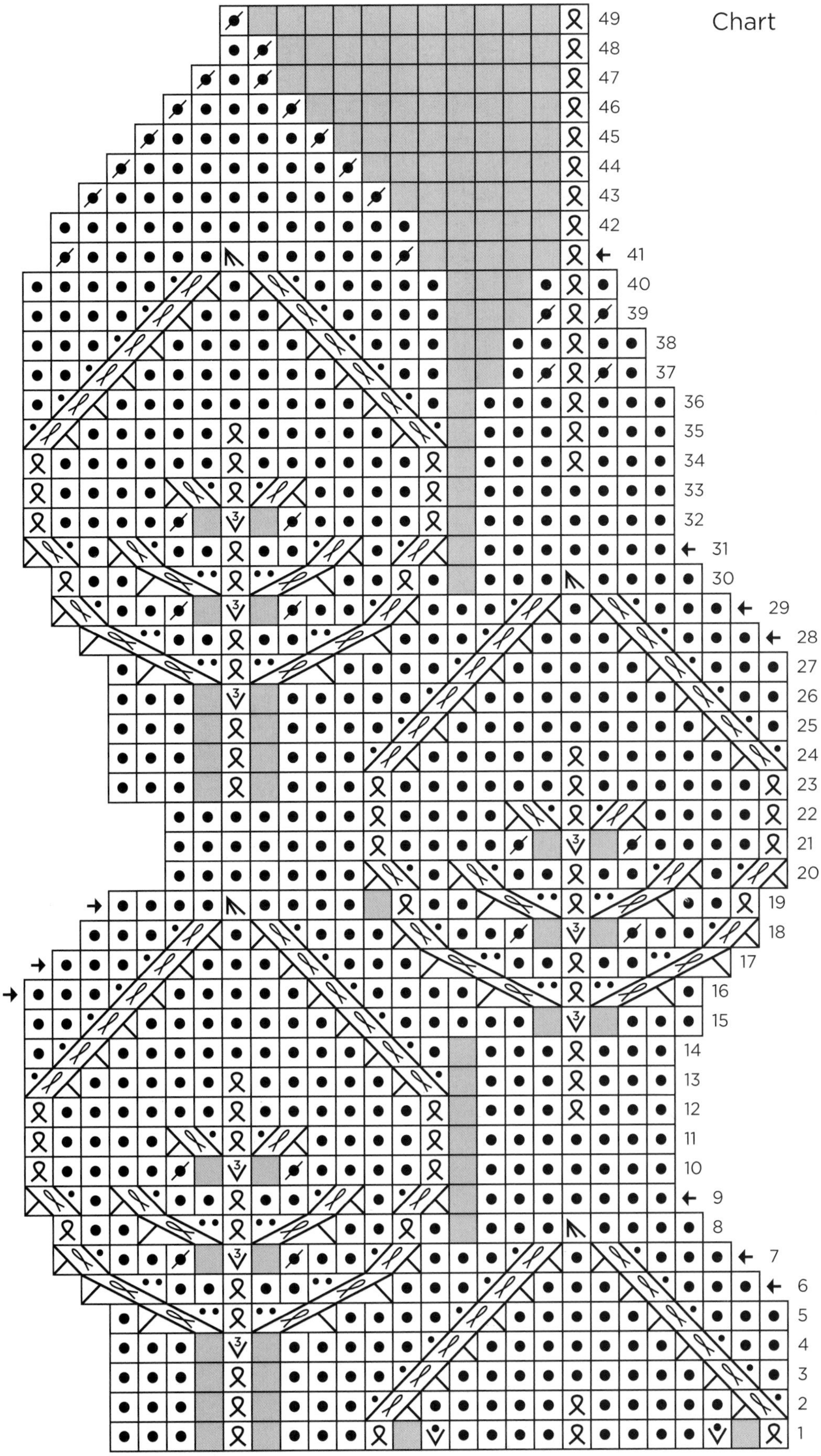

oak trail

A cloche-style hat that sits low and frames the face with a stunning embossed oak leaf gracing one side. The brim is knit flat and then stitches are picked up along one side and knit up in the round to create the body of the hat.

Brim

CO 9 sts onto smaller needle.

Ribbing setup row (WS): P3, k1, p1, k1, p3.
Next row (RS): K3, p1, k1-tbl, p1, k3.

Cont in est rib patt for 4 rows more.

Inc row (WS): P3, kfb, p1, kfb, p3. 11 sts.
Next row (RS): K3, p2, k1-tbl, p2, k3.

Cont in est rib patt for 6 rows more.

Inc row (WS): P3, k1, M1L, k1, p1, k1, M1L, k1, p3. 13 sts.
Next row (RS): K3, p3, k1-tbl, p3, k3.

Cont in est rib patt for 6 rows more.

Inc row (WS): P3, k1, M1L, k2, p1, k2, M1L, k1, p3. 15 sts.
Next row (RS): K3, p4, k1-tbl, p4, k3.

Work even in est rib patt until piece measures approx 10½" / 26 cm
from CO edge. End with a RS row.

Inc row (WS): P3, k4, p1, k2, M1L, k2, p3. 16 sts.

Next row (RS): K3, p5, k1-tbl, p4, k3.

Work even in est rib patt until piece measures approx 19" / 48.5 cm
from CO edge. End with a WS row.

Dec row (RS): K2, ssk, p4, k1-tbl, p4, k3. 15 sts.

Work even in est rib patt until piece measures approx 21" / 53.5 cm
from CO edge. End with a WS row.

Short Row 1 (RS): Work even in est rib patt until 2 sts rem, w&t.
Short Row 2 (WS): Work to end.
Short Row 3 (RS): Work even in est rib patt until 1 st rem before
last wrapped st, w&t.
Short Row 4 (WS): Work to end.

Place safety pin stitch marker at beg of row. Switch to circular needle
and work to end of row, picking up and knitting wraps as you go.

You will now have a long strip of knitted fabric. With RS facing, pick
up and knit 100 sts along all but last ½" / 1.5 cm of left side of strip.
115 sts.

Rnd 1: Join for working in the rnd by sliding last picked up st to left
needle, k3tog. Pm, work chart patt over next 11 sts, pm, k1, M1L,
knit to 15 sts before next marker, pm in alternate color to mark the
beg of the rnd. 114 sts.
Rnds 2-15: Knit to 2 sts before marker, k2tog, sm, work chart patt,
sm, k1, M1L, knit to end. 120 sts after Rnd 15.
Rnd 16: K1, sm, work chart patt, sm, knit to end. 118 sts.
Rnds 17-21: Work to 1 st before marker, M1R, k1, sm, work chart
patt, sm, k1, M1L, knit to end. 116 sts after Rnd 21.

Remove all markers.

Next rnd: K5, Dec-5, pm for new beg of rnd. 112 sts.

Knit 1 rnd.

Work even in St st until work measures 4" / 10 cm from pick-up row.

CROWN DECREASING

Set up rnd: K14, {pm, k14}, rep.

Dec rnd: {K2tog, knit to 2 sts before next marker, ssk}, rep. 16 sts dec.

Rep dec rnd every other rnd 4 times more. Switch to dpns when work
becomes too tight on the circular needle. 32 sts.

Next rnd: {K2tog, ssk}, rep. 16 sts.

Knit 1 rnd. Remove all markers.

Next rnd: Sl 1, pm for new beg of rnd. K2tog 8 times total. 8 sts.

Next rnd: K2tog 3 times total, k2. 5 sts. Remove marker.

Finishing

Cut yarn, thread tail onto tapestry needle, pass through rem 5 sts and cinch to close. Sew rem ½" / 1.5 cm section of brim underneath section marked by safety pin. Left section of brim is now overlapping the full ½" / 1.5 cm.

Weave in all ends on the WS.

Wet block to help keep the brim from rolling.

Chart

□	knit	⊘	p2tog	⚯	M5
⅄	k1-tbl	⋀	S2KP2	⠿	Right Leaf Point: Sl 2 sts to cn and hold to back. Work next 3 sts on needle as follows: K3, turn, p3, turn, S2KP2. Then p2 from cn.
•	purl	ML	M1L	⠿	Left Leaf Point: Sl 3 sts to cn and hold to front, then p2. Work next 3 sts on cn as follows: K3, turn, p3, turn, S2KP2.
╱	k2tog	MR	M1R		
╲	ssk	M	M1-p		

Row 1: K1, p4, k1-tbl, p4, k1.

Row 2: K1, M1-p, p4, M5, p4, M1-p, k1. 17 sts.

Row 3: K1, p5, k5, p5, k1.

Row 4: K1, p5, k2, M1R, k1, M1L, k2, p5, k1. 19 sts.

Row 5: K1, p5, k7, p5, k1.

Row 6: K1, p5, k1, M1R, k2, M1R, k1, M1L, k2, M1L, k1, p5, k1. 23 sts.

Row 7: K1, p5, k11, p5, k1.

Row 8: K1, p3, Right Leaf Point, k5, Left Leaf Point, p3, k1. 19 sts.

Row 9: K1, p2, p2tog, p2, k5, p2, p2tog, p2, k1. 17 sts.

Row 10: K1, p5, {k1, M1R} twice, {k1, M1L} twice, k1, p5, k1. 21 sts.

Row 11: K1, p5, k9, p5, k1.

Row 12: K1, p3, Right Leaf Point, k3, Left Leaf Point, p3, k1. 17 sts.

Row 13: K1, p2, p2tog, p2, k3, p2, p2tog, p2, k1. 15 sts.

Row 14: K1, p5, k1, M1R, k1, M1L, k1, p5, k1. 17 sts.

Row 15: K1, p5, k5, p5, k1.

Row 16: K1, p5, ssk, k1, k2tog, p5, k1. 15 sts.

Row 17: Ssk, p4, k3, p4, k2tog. 13 sts.

Row 18: Ssk, p3, S2KP2, p3, k2tog. 9 sts.

Row 19: Ssk, p5, k2tog. 7 sts.

Row 20: Ssk, p3, k2tog. 5 sts.

Row 21: Ssk, p1, k2tog. 3 sts.

spring foliage

New spring foliage grows up one side and into the thumb gusset of these cozy mitts. Side shaping has been added to flatter the curve of the wrist.

{ SIZE }
Women's Medium

{ FINISHED MEASUREMENTS }
Width: 7" / 18 cm around at widest point of hand
Length: 9½" / 23.5 cm

{ MATERIALS }
2 skeins Berroco *Ultra Alpaca Light* [50% Super Fine Alpaca, 50% Peruvian Wool; 144 yd / 132 m per 1¾ oz / 50g skein] in #4275 Pea Soup Mix OR approx 175 yd / 150 m of a sport or fingering weight alpaca blend

Alternate Yarn: Classic Elite Yarns *Fresco*

Set of US3 / 3.25 mm double-pointed needles

Stitch marker, cable needle, stitch holder, tapestry needle

{ GAUGE }
28 sts and 36 rows over 4" / 10 cm in Reverse St st worked in the rnd on US3 / 3.25 mm needles
Or size needed for accurate gauge.

Cuff

CO 46 sts onto 1 dpn. Divide sts evenly among 3 dpns: 15 sts on 2 needles, 16 sts on 1 needle. Pm, join for working in the rnd being careful not to twist your sts.

Ribbing setup rnd: {K1, p2} 3 times total, {k1, p1} twice, {k1 p2} 11 times total.

Cont in est rib patt for 6 rnds more.

Dec rnd: Work across 8 sts in patt, k2tog, p1, k1, p1, ssk, work in est patt to end. 44 sts.

Cont in est rib patt for 7 rnds more.

Dec rnd: Work across 7 sts in patt, k2tog, p1, k1, p1, ssk, work in est patt to end. 42 sts.

Cont in est rib patt for 7 rnds more.

Dec rnd: Work across 6 sts in patt, k2tog, p1, k1, p1, ssk, work in est patt to end. 40 sts.

Work even in est rib patt until cuff measures 3" / 7.5 cm from CO edge.

Work rnds 1–39 of Chart A.

CREATE THUMB OPENING

Next rnd: P9, {k1, p1} twice, k1, p20, slide next 17 thumb sts onto st holder to be worked later, using backwards loop cast on, CO 1 st, p11. 46 sts.

Next rnd: P9, {k1, p1} twice, k1, p20, k1, p11.

Work even until piece measures 1¾" / 4.5 cm from thumb opening.

Dec rnd: P9, {k1, p1} twice, k1, p9, p2tog, p9, k1, p9, p2tog. 44 sts.
Ribbing set up rnd: {P1, k1}, rep.

Cont in est rib patt for 4 rnds more.

BO in rib. Remove marker. Cut yarn.

Thumb

Return 17 held sts to 1 dpn. Divide thumb sts evenly among 3 dpns. Rejoin yarn.

Work Chart B once.

Ribbing setup rnd: {K1, p1}, rep.

Cont in est rib patt for 1 rnd more.

BO in rib. Remove marker.

Finishing

Cut yarn. Weave in all ends on the WS. Wet block.

Chart A

Rnds 1 & 2: P6, {k1, p1} twice, k1, p17, k1, p11.

Rnd 3: P6, {k1, p1} twice, k1, p17, Inc-3, p11. 42 sts.

Rnd 4: P6, {k1, p1} twice, k1, p15, T3BR, k1, T3FL, p9.

Rnd 5: P5, k2tog, p1, k1, p1, ssk, p14, k1, p2, k1, p2, k1, p9. 40 sts.

Rnd 6: P5, {k1, p1} twice, k1, p12, T3BR, p2, k1, p2, T3FL, p7.

Rnd 7: P5, {k1, p1} twice, k1, p12, {k1, p4} twice, k1, p7.

Rnd 8: P5, {k1, p1} twice, k1, p10, T3BR, p4, k1, p4, T3FL, p5.

Rnd 9: P5, {k1, p1} twice, k1, p10, {k1, p6} twice, k1, p5.

Rnd 10: P5, {k1, p1} twice, k1, p10, Inc-3, p6, k1, p6, Inc-3, p5. 44 sts.

Rnd 11: P5, {k1, p1} twice, k1, p10, k1, p1, k1, {p6, k1} twice, p1, k1, p5.

Rnd 12: P4, k2tog, p1, k1, p1, ssk, p9, k1, yo, p1, yo, {k1, p6} twice, k1, yo, p1, yo, k1, p5. 46 sts.

Rnd 13: P4, {k1, p1} twice, k1, p9, k2, yo, p1, yo, k2,{p6, k1} twice, k1, yo, p1, yo, k2, p5. 50 sts.

Rnd 14: P4, {k1, p1} twice, k1, p9, k3, yo, p1, yo, k3, {p6, k1} twice, k2, yo, p1, yo, k3, p5. 54 sts.

Rnd 15: P4, {k1, p1} twice, k1, p9, k4, p1, k4, {p6, k1} twice, k3, p1, k4, p5.

Rnd 16: P4, {k1, p1} twice, k1, p9, k7, k2tog, p6, Inc-3, p6, ssk, k7, p5.

Rnd 17: P4, {k1, p1} twice, k1, p9, k8, p4, T3BR, k1, T3FL, p4, k8, p5.

Rnd 18: P4, {k1, p1} twice, k1, p9, k6, k2tog, p4, k1,{p2, k1} twice, p4, ssk, k6, p5. 52 sts.

Rnd 19: P4, {k1, p1} twice, k1, p9, k7, p3, T2B, p2, k1, p2, T2F, p3, k7, p5.

Rnd 20: P3, pfb, {k1, p1} twice, k1, pfb, p8, k5, k2tog, p3, Inc-3, p3, k1, p3, Inc-3, p3, ssk, k5, p5. 56 sts.

Rnd 21: P5, {k1, p1} twice, k1, p10, k6, p3, k1, p1, k1, {p3, k1} twice, p1, k1, p3, k6, p5.

Rnd 22: P5, {k1, p1} twice, k1, p10, k4, k2tog, p3, k1, yo, p1, yo, k1, {p3, k1} twice, yo, p1, yo, k1, p3, ssk, k4, p5. 58 sts.

Rnd 23: P4, pfb, {k1, p1} twice, k1, pfb, p9, k5, p3, k2, yo, p1, yo, k2, {p3, k1} twice, k1, yo, p1, yo, k2, p3, k5, p5. 64 sts.

Rnd 24: P6, {k1, p1} twice, k1, p11, k3, k2tog, p3, k3, p1, k3, {p3, k1} twice, k2, p1, k3, p3, ssk, k3, p5. 62 sts.

Rnd 25: P6, {k1, p1} twice, k1, p11, k4, p3, k5, k2tog, p3, k1, p3, ssk, k5, p3, k4, p5. 60 sts.

Rnd 26: P5, pfb, {k1, p1} twice, k1, pfb, p10, k2, k2tog, p3, k6, p3, k1, p3, k6, p3, ssk, k2, p5.

Rnd 27: P7, {k1, p1} twice, k1, p12, k3, p3, k4, k2tog, p3, k1, p3, ssk, k4, p3, k3, p5. 58 sts.

Rnd 28: P7, {k1, p1} twice, k1, p12, S2KP2, p3, k5, p3, Inc-3, p3, k5, p3, S2KP2, p5. 56 sts.

Rnd 29: P6, pfb, {k1, p1} twice, k1, pfb, p10, p2tog, p3, k3, k2tog, p3, k3, p3, ssk, k3, p3, p2tog, p4. 54 sts.

Rnd 30: P8, {k1, p1} twice, k1, p16, k4, p3, {k1, M1-p} twice, k1, p3, k4, p8. 56 sts.

Rnd 31: P8, {k1, p1} twice, k1, p16, k2, k2tog, p3, {k1, pfb} twice, k1, p3, ssk, k2, p8.

Rnd 32: P7, pfb, {k1, p1} twice, k1, pfb, p15, k3, p3, k1, pfb, p1, k1, p1, pfb, k1, p3, k3, p8. 60 sts.

Rnd 33: P9, {k1, p1} twice, k1, p17, S2KP2, p3, k1, p3, Inc-3, p3, k1, p3, S2KP2, p8. 58 sts.

Rnd 34: P9, {k1, p1} twice, k1, p16, p2tog, {p3, k1} twice, p1, {k1, p3} twice, p2tog, p7. 56 sts.

Rnd 35: P9, {k1, p1} twice, k1, p20, k1, p3, k1, yo, p1, yo, k1, p3, k1, p11. 58 sts.

Rnd 36: P9, {k1, p1} twice, k1, p20, k1, p3, k2, p1, k2, p3, k1, p11.

Rnd 37: P9, {k1, p1} twice, k1, p20, k1, pfb, p2, k2, yo, p1, yo, k2, p2, pfb, k1, p11. 62 sts.

Rnd 38: P9, {k1, p1} twice, k1, p20, k1, p4, k3, p1, k3, p4, k1, p11.

Rnd 39: P9, {k1, p1} twice, k1, p20, k1, p4, k7, p4, k1, p11.

Chart B

Rnd 1: K1, p3, pfb, ssk, k3, k2tog, pfb, p3, k1, pick up and knit 1 st on left side of thumb opening, 1 middle st in previous CO, and 1 more st on right side of thumb opening. Pm to mark the beg of rnd. 20 sts.

Rnd 2: K1, p5, ssk, k1, k2tog, p5, {k1, p1} twice. 18 sts.

Rnd 3: K1, p4, pfb, S2KP2, pfb, p4, {k1, p1} twice.

Rnds 4&5: K1, p13, {k1, p1} twice.

☐	knit	⚊	S2KP2			T2B
⦁	purl	○	yo			T2F
╱	k2tog	⩔	pfb			
╲	ssk	M	M1-p			
▨	p2tog	⩔	Inc-3			
▦	no stitch	⎮	place marker			

T3BR: Twist 3 Back Right. Sl 2 sts to cn and hold to back. K1 from left needle, then p2 from cn.

T3FL: Twist 3 Front Left. Sl 1 st to cn and hold to front. P2 from left needle, then k1 from cn.

↓ ↓ ↓ Pick up and knit 1 st on left side of thumb opening, 1 middle st in previous CO, and 1 more st on right side of thumb opening.

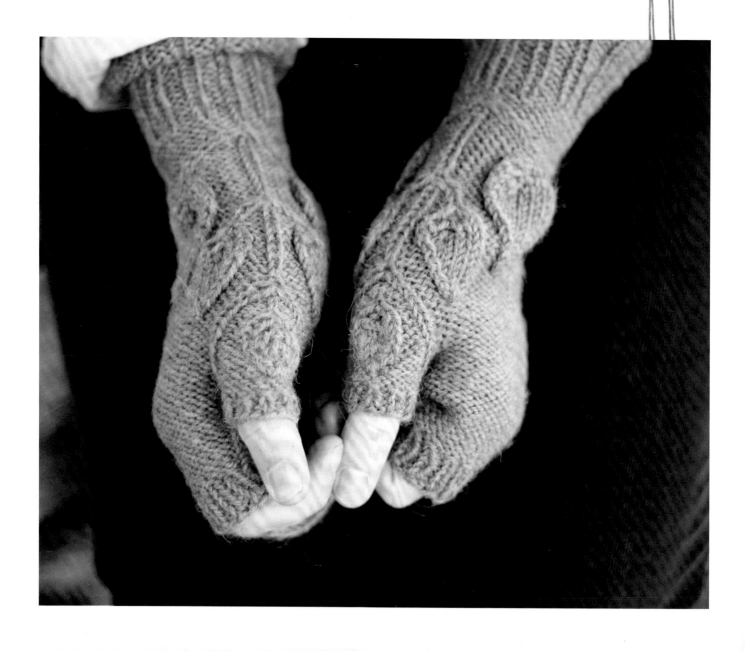

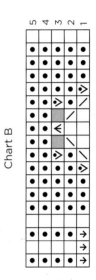

Chart A

Chart B

wrapped in leaves

A larger semi-circular shawl version of my popular *Cedar Leaf Shawlette* to wrap around your shoulders. The scalloped, leafy border is knit on once the body of the shawl is complete.

{ FINISHED MEASUREMENTS }
Length: approx 47" / 119.5 cm from end to end
Width: approx 20" / 51 cm at widest point of center
including border

{ MATERIALS }
4 skeins Classic Elite Yarns *Magnolia* [70% Merino,
30% Silk; 120 yd / 110 m per 1¾ oz / 50 g skein]
in Terra Cotta OR approx 475 yd / 450 m of
a dk weight wool or wool / silk blend

Alternate Yarns: Madelinetosh *Pashmina Worsted*,
Handmaiden *Lady Godiva*

US7 / 4.5 mm 32" / 80 cm circular needle
and 1 double-pointed needle for leaf edging

Stitch markers, tapestry needle

{ GAUGE }
20 sts and 36 rows over 4" / 10 cm in St st
on US7 / 4.5 mm needles
Or size needed for accurate gauge.

Body

CO 3 sts onto circular needle.

Knit 10 rows.

Pick up and knit 5 sts along vertical edge of rectangle in each of the 5 garter st ridges. Pick up and knit 3 sts from CO edge. 11 sts.

Inc row (WS): K3, pfb twice, p1, pfb twice, k3. 15 sts.
Setup row (RS): K3, pm, {k2, pm} twice, k1, {pm, k2} twice, pm, k3.
Next row: K3, purl until 3 sts rem, k3.

Row 1 (RS): K3, {sm, M1R, knit to marker} twice, M1R, sm, k1, sm, M1L, {knit to marker, M1L, sm} twice, k3. 6 sts inc.
Row 2: K3, purl until 3 sts rem, k3.
Row 3: K3, sm, M1R, knit until 3 sts rem, M1L, sm, k3. 2 sts inc.
Row 4: K3, purl until 3 sts rem, k3.

Rep last 4 rows 25 times more, then work rows 1–3 once more. 231 sts.

Purl 1 WS row. Remove markers.

Cut yarn, leaving sts on circular needle.

Leaf Border

With a new ball of yarn, CO 5 sts onto dpn. With RS of shawl facing, use left end of circular needle tip from shawl to work Chart A over sts on dpn.

NOTE: Row 2 and all WS rows end with a p2tog, purling last edging st and next shawl body st together and thus connecting the edging to the knitted fabric as you work.

Work rows 1–22 of Chart A 20 times total. 11 body sts rem.

Work rows 1–22 of Chart B once.

BO rem sts knitwise.

Finishing

Cut yarn. Weave in all ends on the WS. Wet block. Blocking is crucial to the shawl draping well and the leaves lying flat.

Chart A

Row 1 (RS): Sl 1, k1, yo, k1, yo, k2. 7 sts.

Row 2: P6, M1R, p2tog. 8 sts.

Row 3: Sl 1, p1, k2, yo, k1, yo, k3. 10 sts.

Row 4: P8, kfb, p2tog. 11 sts.

Row 5: Sl 1, p2, k3, yo, k1, yo, k4. 13 sts.

Row 6: P10, kfb, k1, p2tog. 14 sts.

Row 7: Sl 1, p3, k4, yo, k1, yo, k5. 16 sts.

Row 8: P12, kfb, k2, p2tog. 17 sts.

Row 9: Sl 1, p4, k5, yo, k1, yo, k6. 19 sts.

Row 10: P14, kfb, k3, p2tog. 20 sts.

Row 11: Sl 1, p5, ssk, k9, k2tog, k1. 18 sts.

Row 12: P12, kfb, k4, p2tog. 19 sts.

Row 13: Sl 1, p6, ssk, k7, k2tog, k1. 17 sts.

Row 14: P10, kfb, k5, p2tog. 18 sts.

Row 15: Sl 1, p1, k1, p5, ssk, k5, k2tog, k1. 16 sts.

Row 16: P8, kfb, k4, p1, k1, p2tog. 17 sts.

Row 17: Sl 1, p1, k1, p6, ssk, k3, k2tog, k1. 15 sts.

Row 18: P6, kfb, k5, p1, k1, p2tog. 16 sts.

Row 19: Sl 1, p1, k1, p7, ssk, k1, k2tog, k1. 14 sts.

Row 20: P4, kfb, k6, p1, k1, p2tog. 15 sts.

Row 21: Sl 1, p1, k1, p8, sk2p, k1. 13 sts.

Row 22: P2tog, BO 7 sts pw, p3, p2tog. 5 sts.

Chart B

Row 1 (RS): Sl 1, k1, yo, k1, yo, k2. 7 sts.

Row 2: P6, M1R, p2tog. 8 sts.

Row 3: Sl 1, p1, k2, yo, k1, yo, k3. 10 sts.

Row 4: P8, kfb, p2tog. 11 sts.

Row 5: Sl 1, p2, k3, yo, k1, yo, k4. 13 sts.

Row 6: P10, kfb, k1, p2tog. 14 sts.

Row 7: Sl 1, p3, k4, yo, k1, yo, k5. 16 sts.

Row 8: P12, kfb, k2, p2tog. 17 sts.

Row 9: Sl 1, p4, k5, yo, k1, yo, k6. 19 sts.

Row 10: P14, kfb, k3, p2tog. 20 sts.

Row 11: Sl 1, p5, ssk, k9, k2tog, k1. 18 sts.

Row 12: P12, kfb, k4, p2tog. 19 sts.

Row 13: Sl 1, p6, ssk, k7, k2tog, k1. 17 sts.

Row 14: P10, kfb, k5, p2tog. 18 sts.

Row 15: Sl 1, p7, ssk, k5, k2tog, k1. 16 sts.

Row 16: P8, kfb, k6, p2tog. 17 sts.

Row 17: Sl 1, p8, ssk, k3, k2tog, k1. 15 sts.

Row 18: P6, kfb, k7, p2tog. 16 sts.

Row 19: Sl 1, p9, ssk, k1, k2tog, k1. 14 sts.

Row 20: P4, kfb, k8, p2tog. 15 sts.

Row 21: Sl 1, p10, sk2p, k1. 13 sts.

Row 22: P2tog, BO 7 sts pw, p3, p2tog. 5 sts.

Chart A

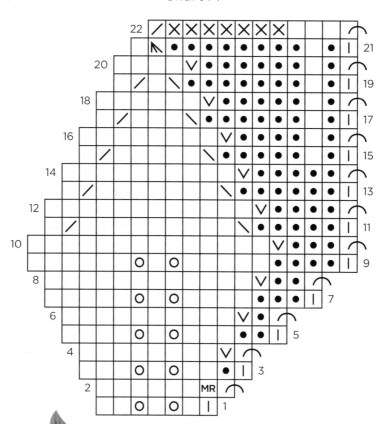

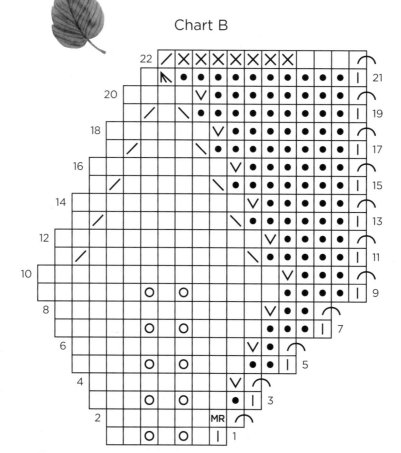

Chart B

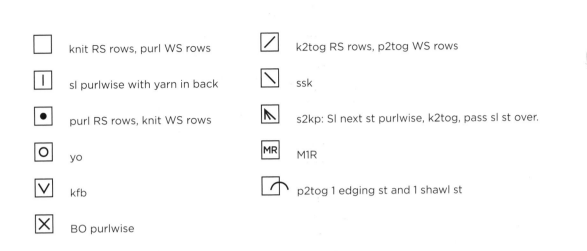

☐	knit RS rows, purl WS rows
☐ (vertical line)	sl purlwise with yarn in back
☐ (dot)	purl RS rows, knit WS rows
☐ (O)	yo
☐ (V)	kfb
☐ (X)	BO purlwise

☐ (/)	k2tog RS rows, p2tog WS rows
☐ (\)	ssk
☐ (↑)	s2kp: Sl next st purlwise, k2tog, pass sl st over.
MR	M1R
☐ (⌒)	p2tog 1 edging st and 1 shawl st

TECHNIQUES

BACKWARDS LOOP CAST ON: Hold the needle in right hand. With left hand, wrap the strand of yarn connected to the ball around thumb counter-clockwise, and hold the strand of yarn loosely in place against the palm of hand with remaining fingers.

*Slip the tip of your needle under the strand of yarn wrapped on the outer-most edge of thumb. The needle will now have an extra loop on it. 1 stitch has been cast on. Tighten up the loop and repeat from * until the needle has the required amount of stitches.

DOUBLE YARN OVER: Wrap yarn clockwise around right needle twice before working the next stitch.

GARTER STITCH: Knit all stitches when working flat. Knit 1 row, purl 1 row when working in the round.

I-CORD: * Knit to end, slide stitches to opposite end of double-pointed needle (do not turn); repeat from *.

KNITTED CAST ON: *Create a knit stitch as you normally would, but before sliding stitch off of left needle, dip left needle underneath and into the loop just created on the right needle. Remove right needle and tighten up the loop. Repeat from * until the needle has the required amount of stitches.

KITCHENER STITCH: Also known as grafting. Thread tail of yarn onto tapestry needle. Place the two double-pointed needles with the remaining stitches next to one another with the wrong sides of the fabric facing in.

Set up: Slide the tapestry needle into the first stitch on the front needle as if to purl. Leave the stitch on the needle and pull the yarn snug. Slide the tapestry needle through the first stitch on the back needle as if to knit. Leave the stitch on the needle and pull the yarn snug.

Step 1: Slide the tapestry needle into the first stitch on the front needle again as if to knit. Pull the yarn snug and this time slide the stitch off of the needle. Slide the tapestry needle into the next stitch on the front needle as if to purl. Leave the stitch on the needle and pull the yarn snug.

Step 2: Slide the tapestry needle into the first stitch on the back needle again as if to purl. Pull the yarn snug and this time slide the stitch off of the needle. Slide the tapestry needle into the next stitch on the back needle as if to knit. Leave the stitch on the needle and pull the yarn snug. Repeat steps 1 and 2 for all stitches.

LONG-TAIL CAST ON: Create a slipknot while leaving a long tail of yarn. Place slipknot onto needle and hold the needle in right hand. With left hand, wrap the strand of yarn attached to the ball around thumb counter-clockwise, and the long tail around index finger clockwise. Hold both strands loosely in place against the palm of hand with remaining fingers.

*Create an opening by slipping the tip of needle under the strand of yarn wrapped on the outer-most edge of thumb. Stretch needle up and over the strand on the inner-most edge of index finger and pull a loop back through the original opening by your thumb. Remove strand of yarn wrapped around thumb. The needle will now have an extra loop on it. 1 stitch has been cast on. Tighten up the loop, return yarn to correct position and repeat from * until the needle has the required amount of stitches.

ONE ROW BUTTONHOLE: Move yarn to front, slip 1 stitch, move yarn to back (slip 1, pass first slipped stitch over the 2nd slipped stitch), repeat once more. Slip last bound-off stitch back to left needle. Turn. With right side facing, cast on 3 stitches using knitted cast on method. Turn. With wrong side facing, move yarn to front, slip 1 stitch, pass last cast-on stitch over the slipped stitch. Slip stitch back to left needle.

PICK UP AND KNIT: Slide needle under both strands of the stitch on the designated edge. Wrap yarn around the needle clockwise and pull a loop through. Repeat across the edge for the required amount of stitches.

REVERSE STOCKINETTE STITCH: Purl on the right side, knit on the wrong side when working flat. Purl all stitches when working in the round.

SHORT ROWS: Also known as wrap and turn (w&t).

Right side or knit stitch: Work in pattern to the stitch to be wrapped, move yarn to front of work and slip next stitch as if to knit. Bring yarn to back and turn work to other side. With wrong side facing, slip same stitch back to right needle as if to purl. Proceed to work across row in pattern.

Wrong side or purl stitch: Work in pattern to the stitch to be wrapped, move yarn to back of work and slip next stitch as if to purl. Bring yarn to front and turn work to other side. With right side facing, slip same stitch back to right needle as if to purl. Proceed to work across row in pattern.

The resulting wrap will look like a "necklace" or "noose" around your stitch.

Picking up wraps: Pull each wrap over to the wrong side of your work as follows:

Right side or knit stitch: Work to previously wrapped stitch. Insert right needle tip under wrap from the bottom up. Pull it up and over the stitch it was wrapping and onto the needle. The wrap will now be behind the stitch on the left needle. Knit both the stitch and the wrap together through the back loop. The wrap should be completely invisible from the right side.

Wrong side or purl stitch: Work to previously wrapped stitch. Insert right hand needle tip under wrap on the right side of your work from the bottom up. (Just as for the right side instructions.) Since the wrong side is facing you, you will have to twist your work to do this. Pull it up and over the stitch it was wrapping towards the wrong side that is facing you and onto the needle. The wrap will now be behind the stitch on the left-hand needle. Purl both the stitch and the wrap together. The wrap should be completely invisible from the right side.

STOCKINETTE STITCH: Knit on the right side, purl on the wrong side when working flat. Knit all stitches when working in the round.

THREE-NEEDLE BIND OFF: Place the two double-pointed needles with the remaining stitches next to one another with the right sides of the fabric facing in. *Slide a 3rd double-pointed needle through the first stitch on the front needle and the first stitch on the back needle as if to knit. Wrap yarn around the needle clockwise and knit through both of these stitches. There is now 1 stitch on the 3rd double-pointed needle. Repeat from * once more. When there are 2 stitches on the 3rd double-pointed needle, lift the first stitch over the second stitch and off of the needle as you would in a normal bind off. Repeat across remaining stitches.

WORK EVEN (AS ESTABLISHED): Work stitches in pattern as they appear without increasing or decreasing.

ABBREVIATIONS

approx: approximately

beg: begin(s)(ning)

BO: Bind Off

C3B: Cable 3 Back. Slip 1 st to cable needle and hold to back. K2 from left needle, then k1 from cable needle.

C3F: Cable 3 Front. Slip 2 sts to cable needle and hold to front. K1 from left needle, then k2 from cable needle.

C4B: Cable 4 Back. Slip 2 sts to cable needle and hold to back. K2 from left needle, then k2 from cable needle.

C4F: Cable 4 Front. Slip 2 sts to cable needle and hold to front. K2 from left needle, then k2 from cable needle.

CO: Cast On

circ: circumference

cont: continue

cm: centimeter(s)

cn: cable needle

dec: decreas(ed)(es)(ing)

Dec-5: Decrease 5. Slip 3 sts with yarn in back. *Pass 2nd st on right needle over the 1st (center st). Slip the center st back to left needle and pass the 2nd st on left needle over it. Slip the center st back to right needle again and rep from * once more. Pick up yarn and knit center st tbl.

Dec-5 pw: Decrease 5 purlwise. Slip 3 sts with yarn in back. *Pass 2nd st on right needle over the 1st (center st). Slip the center st back to left needle and pass the 2nd st on left needle over it. Slip the center st back to

right needle again and rep from * once more. Pick up yarn and purl center st.

dpn(s): double-pointed needle(s)

est: established

inc: increas(ed)(es)(ing)

Inc-3: Increase 3. Knit through the back loop and then through the front loop of the same st. Insert left needle point behind the vertical strand that runs downward between the 2 sts just made and k1-tbl into this strand to make the 3rd st.

k: knit

k1-tbl: knit next st through the back loop

k2tog: Insert needle through next 2 sts as if to knit. Knit together.

k3tog: Insert needle through next 3 sts as if to knit. Knit together.

kfb: knit into front and back of st

M5: Make 5 Increase. ({K1, yo} twice, k1) into 1 st.

m: meters

mm: millimeters

M1R: Make 1 Right Increase. Lift bar between sts from back to front with the left needle and then knit through the front of it with the right needle.

M1, M1L: Make 1 (Left) Increase. Lift bar between sts from front to back with the left needle and then knit through the back of it with the right needle.

M1-p: Make 1 (purlwise) Increase. Lift bar between sts from front to back with the left needle and then purl through the back of it with the right needle.

oz: ounces

patt: pattern(s)

p: purl

p2tog: Insert needle through next 2 sts as if to purl. Purl together.

pfb: purl into front and back of st

pm: place marker

pw: purlwise

rem: remain(s)(ing)

rep: repeat(s)(ing)

rnd(s): round(s)

RS: Right Side

S2KP2: Slip 2 sts together to the right needle as if to knit, knit the next st, then pass the 2 slipped sts over.

sl: slip

sm: slip marker

ssk: slip, slip, knit. Slip 2 sts knitwise, one at a time. Insert left needle through front of sts from left to right and knit together.

sssk: slip, slip, slip, knit. Slip 3 sts knitwise, one at a time. Insert left needle through front of sts from left to right and knit together.

st(s): stitch(es)

St st: Stockinette stitch (see Techniques)

T2B: Twist 2 Back. Slip 1 st to cable needle and hold to back. K1 from left needle, then p1 from cable needle.

T2F: Twist 2 Front. Slip 1 st to cable needle and hold to front. P1 from left needle, then k1 from cable needle.

T3B: Twist 3 Back. Slip 1 st to cable needle and hold to back. K2 from left needle, then p1 from cable needle.

T3F: Twist 3 Front. Slip 2 sts to cable needle and hold to front. P1 from left needle, then k2 from cable needle.

T4B: Twist 4 Back. Slip 2 sts to cable needle and hold to back. K2 from left needle, then p2 from cable needle.

T4F: Twist 4 Front. Slip 2 sts to cable needle and hold to front. P2 from left needle, then k2 from cable needle.

tbl: through the back loop(s)

tog: together

w&t: wrap & turn (see Techniques)

WS: Wrong Side

yd: yards

yo: yarn over

RESOURCES

Brooklyn Tweed *Shelter*
used in *Twigs and Willows*
{ p.36 }

Miss Babs *Yummy Monochrome
Sock & Baby 2-Ply Superwash*
used in *Ivy Trellis Mittens*
{ p.72 }

Quince & Co. *Osprey*
used in *Buds and Blooms*
{ p.24 }

108

Berroco
1 Tupperware Drive, Suite 4
N. Smithfield, RI 02896
401.769.1212
info@berroco.com
berroco.com

Blue Sky Alpacas
P.O. Box 88
Cedar, MN 55011
763.753.5815
info@blueskyalpacas.com
blueskyalpacas.com

Brooklyn Tweed
info@brooklyntweed.net
brooklyntweed.net

Classic Elite Yarns
16 Esquire Road
N. Billerica, MA 01862
800.343.0308
classiceliteyarns.com

**Kelbourne Woolens
(Distributor for
   The Fibre Company)**
2000 Manor Road
Conshohocken, PA 19428
484.368.3666
info@kelbournewoolens.com
kelbournewoolens.com

Madelinetosh
7515 Benbrook Parkway
Benbrook, TX 76126
817.249.3066
info@madelinetosh.com
madelinetosh.com

Miss Babs
P.O. Box 78
Mountain City, TN 37683
423.727.0670
missbabs.com

Quince & Co.
info@quinceandco.com
quinceandco.com

Berroco *Ultra Alpaca Light*
used in *Autumn's End* { p.14 }

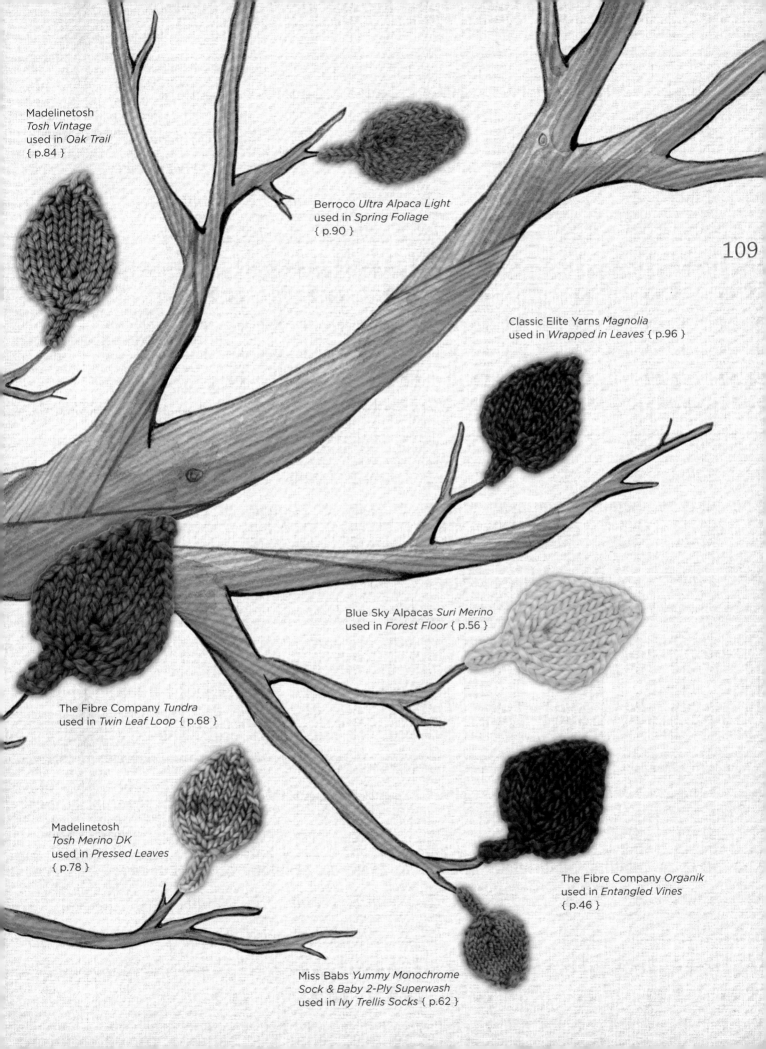

Madelinetosh
Tosh Vintage
used in *Oak Trail*
{ p.84 }

Berroco *Ultra Alpaca Light*
used in *Spring Foliage*
{ p.90 }

109

Classic Elite Yarns *Magnolia*
used in *Wrapped in Leaves* { p.96 }

Blue Sky Alpacas *Suri Merino*
used in *Forest Floor* { p.56 }

The Fibre Company *Tundra*
used in *Twin Leaf Loop* { p.68 }

Madelinetosh
Tosh Merino DK
used in *Pressed Leaves*
{ p.78 }

The Fibre Company *Organik*
used in *Entangled Vines*
{ p.46 }

Miss Babs *Yummy Monochrome
Sock & Baby 2-Ply Superwash*
used in *Ivy Trellis Socks* { p.62 }

A BIG THANK YOU to all of the knitters who have supported Never Not Knitting

acknowledgments

A special thank you to the following contributors who lent their talent, expertise and time to this project. I could not have done it without you.

Graphic Design by Mary Joy Gumayagay (indus3ous.com)

Technical Editing by Tana Pageler and Dawn Catanzaro

Illustration by Neesha Hudson (neeshahudson.com)

Photography by Carlee Tatum (prettyminded.com)

Modeling by Courtney Riddle

Test knitting by Andrea Sanchez, Anne Ginger, Chauntel Sedgwick Ensey, Deb Barnhill, Helen Gavel, Peter Kennedy, Rebecca Swafford, Sarah Cote, Tana Pageler and Veronika Jobe

Copy Editing by Nicole Crosby (thefinalwordediting.com)

As always, thank you to my husband, Jason, for your continued support.

And thank you to my friend Tamarie Rayner for your ideas and assistance during our photoshoot.

from the very first pattern to this latest self-published book!

little leaves

These little leaves have many uses. Sew them onto knitted items as appliques, use them as bookmarks, or string several together for a crib mobile, wreath or wall hanging. The possibilities are endless!

NOTE: This pattern can be knit with the yarn of your choice. Gauge is not important. Be sure to use the appropriate size needle for your yarn thickness.

Have fun!

CO 3 sts. Work in I-cord for 6 rnds total. Turn. **Row 1 (WS):** P3.
Row 2 (RS): K1, M1R, p1, M1L, k1. 5 sts. **Row 3:** P2, k1, p2.
Row 4: K1, M1R, k1, M1R, p1, M1L, k1, M1L, k1. 9 sts.
Row 5: P4, k1, p4. **Row 6:** K4, M1R, p1, M1L, k4. 11 sts. **Row 7:** P5, k1, p5.
Row 8: Knit. **Row 9:** Purl. **Row 10:** Knit. **Row 11:** Purl.
Row 12: Ssk, knit until 2 sts rem, k2tog. 9 sts.
Row 13: Purl. Rep last 2 rows 4 times more. 3 sts.
Next row: S2KP2. Cut yarn. Fasten off
and weave in ends on the WS.